THE RESURRECTION OF THE DEAD.

THE RESURRECTION OF THE DEAD

AN EXPOSITION OF 1 CORINTHIANS XV.

BY THE LATE

WILLIAM MILLIGAN, D.D.

PROFESSOR OF DIVINITY AND BIBLICAL CRITICISM IN THE
UNIVERSITY OF ABERDEEN

SECOND EDITION

WIPF & STOCK · Eugene, Oregon

Wipf and Stock Publishers
199 W 8th Ave, Suite 3
Eugene, OR 97401

The Resurrection of the Dead
An Exposition of 1 Corinthian XV
By Milligan, William
ISBN 13: 978-1-60608-438-0
Publication date 01/09/2009
Previously published by T & T Clark, 1895

Prefatory Note.

The following chapters appeared originally in *The Monthly Interpreter* and *The Expositor*. They are now republished in accordance with what is known to have been the writer's intention.

G. M.

March 1894.

CONTENTS.

CHAPTER		PAGE
I.	1 Cor. xv. 1-11	3
II.	1 Cor. xv. 12-19	21
III.	1 Cor. xv. 20-22	41
IV.	1 Cor. xv. 23-28	61
V.	1 Cor. xv. 29-32a	79
VI.	1 Cor. xv. 32b-34	97
VII.	1 Cor. xv. 35-41	117
VIII.	1 Cor. xv. 42-44	139
IX.	1 Cor. xv. 45, 46	161
X.	1 Cor. xv. 47-49	181
XI.	1 Cor. xv. 50-52	199
XII.	1 Cor. xv. 53-58	225

"Now I make known unto you, brethren, the gospel which I preached unto you, which also ye received, wherein also ye stand, by which also ye are saved; I make known, I say, in what words I preached it unto you, if ye hold it fast, except ye believed in vain. For I delivered unto you first of all that which also I received, how that Christ died for our sins according to the scriptures; and that he was buried; and that he hath been raised on the third day according to the scriptures; and that he appeared to Cephas; then to the twelve; then he appeared to above five hundred brethren at once, of whom the greater part remain until now, but some are fallen asleep; then he appeared to James; then to all the apostles; and last of all, as unto one born out of due time, he appeared to me also. For I am the least of the apostles, that am not meet to be called an apostle, because I persecuted the church of God. But by the grace of God I am what I am: and his grace which was bestowed upon me was not found vain; but I laboured more abundantly than they all: yet not I, but the grace of God which was with me. Whether then it be I or they, so we preach, and so ye believed."—1 COR. xv. 1-11. [R.V.]

THE
RESURRECTION OF THE DEAD.

Chapter i.

IN entering upon the effort to explain and illustrate the course of St. Paul's argument in the fifteenth chapter of the First Epistle to the Corinthians, it may be well, in the meantime, to postpone any inquiry into the peculiar views of those with whom the Apostle has to contend. We shall be able to form more correct ideas upon this point either in the course of our exposition of the chapter, or when we have brought it to a close. It is enough to observe now, that the whole character of the Apostle's reasoning shows how deeply moved he himself was by the thought of the momentous subject with which he is to deal. His very first word—" I make known " is one of power —*Antea fuerat doctrina*, says Bengel, *nunc fit elenchus*. It is the word which he had used in chap. xii. 3, when the awful thought of calling Jesus *Anathema* was present to his mind. More than that, it is the word used by our Lord Himself when, in the last sentence of His high-priestly prayer, He thought of the Divine authority with which, as the revelation of the Father, He had impressed the knowledge of the Father upon the hearts of the disciples, so that in them the end of His coming had been answered, " that the love wherewith Thou lovest Me may be in them, and I in them" (John xvii. 26). " I make known " is more than I announce, or declare, or preach, or call to mind. It carries with it the whole weight of St. Paul's apostolical authority, as well as the remembrance of that submission which the Corinthian Christians had formerly yielded to his words. As, too, with the first word of the chapter, so also with the tone of the chapter throughout. There is an animation, a fervour, a swing in it almost unexampled even in the writings of one whose letters were " weighty and strong." Seldom does even he rise to such impassioned thought, such ardent feeling, or such lofty eloquence. He is evidently contending for what he knows to be one of the most central truths of that Gospel which he had received by direct communication from heaven. With it were connected all perseverance and enthusiasm in the work of the Lord (ver. 58). Without it the whole substance of his message disappeared (ver. 14), and its fruits perished (ver. 17).

The subject of the chapter is the Resurrection of the Dead. In the days when that great truth was first proclaimed, men questioned and denied it as they questioned and denied hardly any other doctrine which Jesus or His Apostles preached. No belief of the early Church roused to such an extent the indignation of the Sadducees, the most powerful party in Jerusalem at the time (Acts iv. 2). It was received with mockery at Athens and throughout the Gentile world (Acts xvii. 32). One of the earliest heresies that sprang up in the bosom of the Christian Church itself, was that of Hymenæus and Philetus, who maintained that the resurrection was past already, and overthrew the faith of some (2 Tim. ii. 18). At Corinth, as we learn from this chapter, there were those in the midst of the Christian community who denied the doctrine, and asked either in perplexity or scorn, "How are the dead raised, and with what manner of body do they come?" (ver. 35).

But if there was difficulty in believing in the resurrection of the dead then, the difficulty is one which has only increased with time. The lapse of centuries has placed many another doctrine of our faith in a clearer and brighter light, and has made it easier of acceptance than it was at the beginning. It is not so here. As ever enlarging multitudes return to the dust, and the particles of their bodies enter in other forms into the frames of generations that follow them, the mind becomes bewildered in its effort to imagine what the resurrection of the dead can mean. How often do we torture ourselves with the thought of it! How often would we fain pause and dismiss the whole subject as one of those impenetrable mysteries which it is useless at present to endeavour to comprehend! But there is no pausing on the part of the Apostle in the chapter before us. On the contrary, the whole tenor of the chapter shows that he is animated in a higher than ordinary degree by the confidence, the assurance, the joy, of faith. He feels that he is entering into the very heart of the Christian system. He seems almost to experience a sensation of relief as he turns from many of the points with which, in the earlier part of his Epistle, he had been engaged. The factions, the lawsuits, the disputes about meats, articles of dress, and gifts had wearied him. Now he is in his element, and he rushes like a war-horse to the battle.

In the first paragraph of the chapter, extending from ver. 1 to ver. 11, the foundation of the Apostle's argument is laid, and it may be summed up in the single sentence, "The Christ who died is risen." The Corinthian Christians indeed did not doubt that fact. Even those among them who hesitated to admit that there was any prospect of a resurrection for themselves, did not deny that, on the third morning after His crucifixion, their Lord had come forth in triumph from the grave. The proclamation of that great truth had, most of all, made them Christians. It had confirmed in the most wonderful and striking way the highest claims put forth by One who to the outward eye had no form, nor comeliness, and no beauty that men should desire Him. It had authenticated in a manner which no human reasoning could overthrow, His assertion that He was the Son of God, and the Sent of God to be the Saviour of the world. It had illustrated the nature of that imperishable life which He Himself possessed, and which He communicated to all who identified themselves with Him. It had shown with what approbation and honour the Almighty regarded One who had been persecuted to a shameful death. It had surrounded the very cross of Calvary with glory. The early Christians in general, and no doubt the Corinthian Christians along with them, knew well that the Church of Christ had not been founded only upon a Saviour who died, but upon One who, though crucified in weakness, had been raised by the power of God; and the life which they lived was life in a risen Lord. Therefore it is that, whatever the doubts they might entertain with regard to their own resurrection, the chapter before us affords not the slightest intimation that they entertained any with regard to the Resurrection of Jesus.

Yet, although this was the case, St. Paul feels that it was of the utmost importance to restate the truths already in their minds, and to impress these truths upon them with renewed power. The difference is vast between acknowledging that a thing is true, and seeing that truth stand out before our eyes in the clearness of deep and deliberate conviction. In the former case the truth may have no possession of us. It may be in our minds like seed laid up in a storehouse, retaining indeed the principle of life, and ready for use at some future day, but as yet without vigour or result. In the latter case it is like seed cast into a soil which contains all the appropriate conditions for its growth, and to which it is no sooner committed than it begins to sprout, and to send up first the blade, and then the ear, and then the full corn in the ear. Would we know the power of any truth that we have believed, we need to be constantly returning to it, constantly renewing our acquaintance with it, constantly satisfying ourselves, amidst all the fresh experiences that we make, of its reality and value.

Hence it is that, before entering upon the special argument of this chapter, St. Paul states again the substance of his Gospel, and that in such a way as ought to have awakened the most tender and powerful impressions in connection with it.

1. *First*, he reminds the Corinthian Christians of the contents of that Gospel which he had preached at Corinth. These contents are contained in the verses extending from ver. 3 to ver. 8, and the double introduction of the words "according to the Scriptures" gives the key to the arrangement of the particulars mentioned. In the first place, these are four in number, divided into two groups, the first group embracing the facts that the Lord Jesus Christ died for our sins and was buried; the second, that He rose from the grave on the third day and that He appeared after His Resurrection to the persons named. In the second place, the words "according to the Scriptures" show us, from the manner in which they are introduced, not only that we are dealing with two groups of facts, but that the chief stress of the statement is laid upon the first of the two particulars mentioned in each group,—"Christ died for our sins according to the Scriptures, and," etc.; "He hath been raised on the third day according to the Scriptures, and,"

etc. In other words, the Gospel preached by St. Paul consisted mainly of the two great truths that Christ died for our sins and that He rose again. The other two are subordinate and subsidiary. That Christ was "buried" is no doubt even in itself full of consolation to the Christian mind, not simply because, as commentators so often think, it attests His death or prepares the way for His Resurrection, but because it illustrates His complete identification of Himself with all the different stages of our human history. Not only did He pass through life and death before us, He passed also through that grave in which we must one day be laid in a solitude upon which no friend of earth can break. That after His Resurrection Christ appeared to Cephas and the others who are here mentioned, is likewise of the utmost importance; for it assures us that, in accepting the crowning doctrine of our faith, we are following no cunningly-devised fable or fond delusion, but are dealing with a fact established by most abundant and varied evidence. Yet, important as these two points may be, they are not themselves the substance of the Gospel. That substance is to be found in the two immediately preceding them —Christ died for our sins, and rose again on the third day.

Even this, however, is not all. The words "rose again" of the Authorized Version do not bring out the meaning of the original. We ought to read, with the Revised Version, "hath been raised;" and the difference between the two renderings, though the latter may be unmarked, or, when it is marked, may be blamed by many, is one of those differences that carry with them a whole world of theology. The reading "rose again" tells us only that on the third morning Jesus burst the bonds of death, and came forth victorious from the grave, a conqueror over it in His own Divine and triumphant might. The reading "hath been raised" tells us that He not only rose, but that in the state in which He rose He continued when the Apostle wrote, and by parity of reasoning continues still. It conveys to us the assurance that He did not die again, but that having died once He dieth no more: death hath no more dominion over Him. He lives, unchangeably the same, for ever.

And now we see what the two leading points of St. Paul's Gospel were. In conformity with the whole teaching of Scripture, they were these,—first, Christ died for our sins; secondly, He hath been raised and He lives for ever. These truths may not be separated from each other. God hath joined them together: no man may put them asunder. They include the whole history of Christ from His Incarnation onward; and because they include His history, they include also that of His people. Without the first the second would bring little comfort to us in our sinfulness. Even supposing for a moment (what, however, the Apostle afterwards declares to be impossible) that Christ had passed through the grave to a glorious Resurrection without our being concerned in His work, it is conceivable that we might have no part with Him in that Resurrection. Looked at in itself, it might convey to us no earnest or foretaste of our own. Because He rose who was the Only-begotten of the Father, who did always and perfectly the Father's will, and in whom the Father was always well pleased, it would not follow that we who had violated the Divine commandments, and in whose case death was not a mere transition stage to life, should also rise. It is Christ's dying for our sins as our Representative, which gives us hope that, partakers of His death, we shall also be partakers of His Resurrection. Without the second truth, again, the first would be of as little avail. "If Christ hath not been raised," says St. Paul in the seventeenth verse of the chapter, "your faith is vain; ye are yet in your sins,"—words which do not mean simply that our sins are not forgiven us, but that we must still be living in sin as the element of our whole moral being. It is in Christ the risen Saviour that we are introduced into that new and higher and heavenly life in which we are to walk; and except when brought into that life, the life which can alone satisfy the desires and complete the glory of our nature, we cannot be at peace. Thus the death and Resurrection of Christ must always go together as two sides of one compound truth. The separation too often made between them in theology is not found in the writings of St. Paul.

Upon the details of the manifestations of Himself by the Risen Lord, contained in the verses extending from ver. 5 to ver. 8, it does not seem necessary to dwell. One or two points, however, may be briefly noticed. (1) The word "appeared" must denote actual and bodily appearances of the Risen Saviour, and not visions of the mental eye. We know from the Gospels that it was thus that Christ appeared in several of the instances here recorded, and the sense of the word applicable to some must be applied to all. The use of the word too in 1 Tim. iii. 16, "appeared to angels" (not "seen of angels," as in the Authorized and Revised Versions), is conclusive upon the point. Angels surely do not see visions. (2) All the appearances recorded belong to a date anterior to the conversion of the Apostle. No hesitation can be felt upon this point except in the case of that mentioned in ver. 8, the appearance to St. Paul himself. Yet the words in which the Apostle designates himself as the τὸ ἔκτρωμα ("the one born out of due time") of the apostolic band, hardly admit of any other interpretation. St. Paul felt, as he tells us in the next following verse, connected with that preceding by the word "for," that he was the least of the Apostles, and that he was not meet to be called an Apostle, *because he persecuted the Church of God*. Therefore it was that he deserves to be called the ἔκτρωμα "the abortion," among the rest, and the time which suggested such a humiliating name was that when he was yet a persecutor. (3) The words "last of all" in ver. 8, when viewed in their relation to the several times repeated ἔπειτα ("then") of the previous verses, seem distinctly to imply that the manifestation spoken of was not only the last of the particular series to which allusion had been made, and which might therefore have been afterwards renewed, but that it was the final appearance of the Risen Lord in the form and way then in question. (4) There is difficulty in determining the principle upon which the different appearances of the Risen Christ, here gathered together by St. Paul, are grouped. The mention of " the twelve " in ver. 5, compared with that of " all the Apostles " in ver. 7, is sufficient to show that the arrangement is not chronological. It would seem rather that the whole number is divided into two groups, each consisting of three members. The first group will then have special relation to Christ's disciples in their home life, and that in three rising gradations—Peter, the twelve, the five hundred, all of these being viewed in their personal relation to Jesus; the second to the disciples looked at in their action on the world, again in three rising gradations—James the head of the Church at Jerusalem, all the Apostles (sent out upon their mission), the Apostle of the Gentiles.

Once more, before passing from that aspect of the two great truths of these verses, Christ's death and His endless life after death, which we are now considering, it may be well to notice that these truths embody not facts alone, but facts accomplished through the eternal purpose of God. Such is the meaning of the words " according to the Scriptures " associated with each. For, when he thus speaks, it is no mere fulfilment of prophecy that is in the Apostle's mind.

He does not wish merely to tell us that, hundreds of years before the events took place, the death and Resurrection of Jesus had been foretold by prophets, and that in the fulfilment of their predictions, in the correspondence of event with prophecy, we have an assurance that we are dealing not with mistaken traditions but with actual fact. He refers to the Scriptures, and the mention made in them of these things, for a different purpose. These Scriptures were the expression of the Divine will. They were the record of the Divine doings. They were the revelation of the Divine purposes. What they contained was either a statement or an illustration of the unchangeable principles of the Divine economy.

When, accordingly, we find the death and the life after death of the coming Redeemer spoken of in the Scriptures with gradually increasing clearness as the time for their accomplishment drew nigh, we are invited to think of them as far more than a simple fulfilment of prophecy. They are a part of the execution of God's great plan. They have their place in the Divine administration of the universe. They are not a scheme devised by man, or angel, or even by the Son Himself, to procure redemption for us. In them God accomplishes His own ends. He sent the Son. He so " loved the world as to give His only-begotten Son, that whosoever believeth in Him should not perish, but have eternal life."

2. *Secondly*, the object of the Apostle in these introductory verses of the chapter is not merely to tell

the Corinthian Christians the contents of that Gospel which he preached, as he had often told it them before. His aim is so to tell it that they shall be reminded of its power, and be thus the better prepared for the important consequences to be connected with it in the subsequent portion of the chapter. Hence, accordingly, he reminds them—

(1) That it was this Gospel which had first awakened them to spiritual life. "Now I make known unto you," he says in verse 1, not only "the Gospel which I preached unto you," but "which also ye received." He takes them back to the moment when he had first come among them as the Apostle of a Risen Lord, and when by the tidings which he preached they had been first led to faith. What a moment never to be forgotten had that been! In their fair and beautiful city they had been cultivating their philosophy, and it had failed to satisfy either the questionings of the intellect or the longings of the heart. The wisest teachers of the day had been at their command, but they "through wisdom knew not God" (chap. i. 21). Idolatry in its most debasing forms, heathenism with its most impure and degrading rites, prevailed on every side. Then the Apostle came. He had been persecuted in Thessalonica. He had been driven from Berœa. He had been compelled to leave Athens, and it was with the marks of suffering upon him that he had arrived at Corinth. But the opposition that he had met with had only roused his spirit. The Lord had appeared

to him in the night by a vision, and had said, "Be not afraid, but speak, and hold not thy peace: for I am with thee, and no man shall set on thee to hurt thee; for I have much people in this city" (Acts xviii. 9, 10); he had obeyed the vision, and had continued there a year and six months teaching the word of God among them, with what success they could themselves best testify.

These were affecting memories,—affecting to St. Paul, not less affecting to the Corinthian Christians; and they were all brought up by the words "which also ye received." Well, then, is the Apostle's argument, ye remember that spring-time of your spiritual life, and that the truth which then produced the change was that regarding a Redeemer who had passed through death to everlasting and glorious life, and whom I could then proclaim to you as the Risen and Living Lord. Surely you will think of that truth now as one to be held fast in faith. Not only so—

(2) The Apostle reminds them that this was the truth which from that moment until now had maintained their spiritual life in vigour. "Wherein also," he says, ver. 2, "ye stand." He had not only the past to appeal to, but the present, the multiplied evidences of Divine grace that could be seen, the manifold fruits of the Christian life that were exhibited, among them. In no early Christian church were these results so conspicuous as in Corinth. Nowhere did they find so rich a soil from which to spring. The life of the

Corinthian Christians was fuller and more striking than in any other city of the time.

Again, therefore, the appeal is to the same purpose as before. I do not send you, says the Apostle, only to the past. I bid you look at what you have continued to be down to this very hour. Notwithstanding all your shortcomings and sins, you know that you have a Divine life among you, a life that connects you with God and a higher world than the present. By what is it maintained? Is it not by that very Gospel which I preached at first, that we have a Lord who has passed through death to His exaltation at the right hand of God? He it is who supplies from His own living presence what keeps you alive. Because He is with you alway, you are what you are. Surely you will think of that truth now as one to be held fast in faith. Once more—

(3) St. Paul connects this faith with the attainment of a full salvation. " By which also," he says in ver. 2, " ye are saved," or rather, however unpleasant the English may be, " ye are being saved :" that is, by which also ye are receiving larger measures of salvation, and shall at last obtain the full salvation for which ye wait and long. The salvation spoken of is not to be understood in the sense of mere deliverance from the penalty of sin, in the theological sense of justification. We shall fail to comprehend the root of the Apostle's reasoning if we identify these two, as if the man who is justified were also saved, or the man who

is saved were no more than justified. Salvation is a far wider word than justification. It includes not pardon only but spiritual life, deliverance of the soul from the power not less than the punishment of sin, restoration to the Divine image, conformity of character to the inheritance of the saints in light. And whence is the hope of this salvation obtained? Not simply from the death of Christ. There we may obtain pardon for past offences. There we may feel that our sins are covered in the blood of Him who, as our Representative, took upon Him death for us. But there we have not, nor in the nature of the case can we have, life. Life flows from life. It may spring up in the midst of death, but not from death. It is a Living Lord who quickens us to be partakers of His own life. Christian hope is more than the hope of deliverance from sorrow or crying or pain. It is first and most of all the hope of deliverance from sin, to be no more tempted to evil either from within or from without, to be like the Lord when we see Him as He is. Surely we ought to think of this truth also as one to be held fast in faith.

Such is the statement with which the Apostle opens the argument of this chapter. It is a statement of fact and an appeal to experience. There is undoubtedly proof presented of the fact that Christ rose from the grave. But there could be no proof by witnesses who could be seen and questioned, that Christ was living still at the right hand of the Father an endless life of glory. For that the Corinthian

Christians must depend upon positive assertion confirmed by undeniable experience of the result. Even the witnesses of the Resurrection of Christ are cited less as witnesses to prove a point, than as witnesses who tell an old story over again in order to revivify the convictions of their hearers. St. Paul is not dealing with sceptics as to the Resurrection of the Lord to whom it is necessary to present a proof, but with persons whose eyes were only becoming dim to it, and their hearts insensible to its influence. All, both Apostle and converts, are agreed upon one point, and have one point to start from. The Christ who had died and risen again, who had passed through death to life, was the substance of their common faith. Whether it was St. Paul himself or his fellow-Apostles, so they preached, and so the Corinthians believed. Let the latter think over it again; and, as they were even now persuaded of the truth itself, let them be prepared to follow it out, as they would follow out all truth, to the consequences which were legitimately involved in it.

"*Now if Christ is preached that he hath been raised from the dead, how say some among you that there is no resurrection of the dead? But if there is no resurrection of the dead, neither hath Christ been raised: and if Christ hath not been raised, then is our preaching vain, your faith also is vain. Yea, and we are found false witnesses of God; because we witnessed of God that he raised up Christ: whom he raised not up, if so be that the dead are not raised. For if the dead are not raised, neither hath Christ been raised: and if Christ hath not been raised, your faith is vain; ye are yet in your sins. Then they also which are fallen asleep in Christ have perished. If in this life only we have hoped in Christ, we are of all men most pitiable.*"—1 COR. xv. 12-19. [R.V.]

Chapter ii.

IN the first eleven verses of the chapter the Apostle had laid the foundation of his argument, and he is now ready to proceed to the argument itself. He is to conduct it by an appeal to what the Corinthian Christians knew and acknowledged with regard to the Resurrection and the Resurrection-life of Christ. Neither of these great facts is he again to establish. Even the witnesses, cited in the long list contained in vers. 5-8 of the chapter, had been cited by him not so much to prove what hardly stood in need of proof, as to illustrate and enforce the fact on which his mind was fixed, and to bring it home to his readers with fresh liveliness and power. To this last result all that he had said had tended; and now the result is gained. The Risen and glorified Redeemer is before both himself and the Corinthian Church as One who, after having died for their sins, has been raised from the grave, and has ascended to His Father and their Father, to His God and their God. Having gained this point St. Paul is ready to proceed with his argument for the resurrection of the dead. It is drawn from the absurd and incredible consequences involved in a denial of the fact, and it is summed up in one particular, everything that follows being merely subsidiary to this : " Now, if Christ is preached that He hath been raised from the dead, how say some among you that there is no resurrection of the dead ? But if there is no resurrection of the dead, neither hath Christ been raised."

The conclusion was obvious and direct. It was urged at Corinth that the resurrection of the dead was impossible. Once committed to the grave, was the plea, all experience shows that the body returns to the dust from which it was originally taken; its particles mingle with the particles of the soil in which it finds its final resting-place; nay, they even pass from that soil into other forms of vegetable and animal existence; they cannot be gathered together again, and be built up in their old earthly frame; if we are to use the word resurrection at all, we must apply it to the spiritual resurrection which takes place when we believe in Christ, and are made new creatures in Him. You yourself, the objectors would further urge, have taught us to look at the matter in this light. You have said that when a sinner embraces the offer of the gospel he dies, and that his life is thenceforward hid with Christ in God. More than that, you have said that, in the first great open crisis of his spiritual history, he is buried with Christ through baptism into death, that, like as Christ was raised from the dead through the glory of the Father, so also he might walk in newness of life. That is the only resurrection. There is no resurrection from the grave. Our proposition to that effect is universal, and it cannot be disputed.

But, if so, it followed as a necessary consequence that Christ had not been raised. Christ did not come into the world as an exception to the laws that regulate the ordinary history of man, or to occupy a position entirely separate and distinct from that of the other members of the human family. He did not come to show us in His life and death and Resurrection and Ascension what an order of beings wholly distinct from man might be, might do, or might become. It is true that He was the Son of God, but He was also the Son of man, possessed of a genuine and complete humanity, so that whatever befell Him may befall us, that whatever is inconsistent with the essential, although it may be the undeveloped, powers of humanity was not less to Him impossible.

If, therefore, it be a law pertaining to the essence of human nature that one who has once died shall never rise from the dead, we must be deceived in our belief of Christ's Resurrection; He hath not, He cannot have, been raised. It is unnecessary to argue the point further. There were only two ways in which the conclusion could be escaped. Either Christ was not truly man, or He had not been raised. The doubters at Corinth would accept neither alternative. They believed that Christ was truly man. They believed not less that He at least had been raised. Their universal proposition was shown in a particular.

instance to be false, and they were bound therefore, if they reasoned correctly, to abandon it.

The Apostle, however, had been accustomed to argue, not only with hesitating or heretical Christians, but with stubborn Jews and Greek philosophers who had all the sophistry of the day at their command. He knew therefore that a mere victory in argument was not enough. Even if convinced that he was right, and unable to reply, his hearers might so cling to their original position that, rather than abandon it, they might be tempted to modify the conditions under which they held it, and to doubt whether, after all, Christ *was* risen. If, they might say, the Resurrection of Christ and the resurrection of the dead are so inseparably bound up with one another, may we not have made some mistake in the mode in which we have clung to our belief in the latter fact? We see no way of forsaking our first proposition, that a resurrection of the dead there cannot be. What if we should be compelled by the necessities of logical defence to admit that Christ Himself did not rise?

Such is the danger that the Apostle has now before him; and accordingly he meets it by pointing out several consequences that will flow from an acceptance of the possibility that the Resurrection of Christ had not really taken place.

1. "If Christ hath not been raised, then is our preaching" (not the act of preaching, but the substance of what was preached) " vain, your faith

also is vain." (ver. 14); and again (ver. 17), " your faith is vain." In these two verses the " vanity " spoken of is expressed by two different words, the one (κενός) denoting what has no reality, what is empty or void, the other (μάταιος) denoting what produces no effect, what issues in no good; while, in the latter verse of the two, the Apostle brings his meaning still more fully out by adding to the words " your faith is vain," " ye are yet in your sins." His meaning therefore is obvious. If Christ has not been raised, and is not now a living Lord, the gospel which we preach is a meaningless proclamation to men ; it has no reality, no power to bring them deliverance ; they are yet in their sins.

But what is the connexion between these two facts ? Does St. Paul mean simply to tell us this, that if Christ has not been raised it is a proof that the burden of our sins has been too much for Him ; that even by His life and labours and sufferings and death He has failed to expiate sin ; that our sins are still around Him and upon Him in that grave to which He had been committed ; that He has not accomplished the atonement for which we hoped ; and that we are still under the curse of the law, with nothing before us but a certain fearful looking for of judgment and fiery indignation, from which there is no prospect of escape ? This may be in part his meaning ; but when it is presented to us as the whole, it is unsatisfactory and incomplete. It is at variance with that teaching of Scripture which tells us that not death, but life through death, was the end for which Jesus came; it makes the pardon of sin the main purpose of the Divine economy of grace; and it resolves the Resurrection of Christ into a mere proof that His death has been accepted by the Almighty as an all-sufficient offering upon our behalf. Besides which, it is hardly possible, under this point of view, to understand the force of the Apostle's argument. If Christ came into the world simply to die for us, and thereby to procure us acceptance with God; if He did die a spotless and acceptable victim to that righteous Lawgiver whose holiness we had offended, and whose law we had outraged; if, according to His own language, recorded by St. John, the love of the Father was most of all drawn out to Him by the fact that He laid down His life (John x. 17), it is not easy to see why His death should have been in vain, even although He did not rise. Why should His sacrifice not have been complete when upon the cross of Calvary He came to the termination of His woe? Without His Resurrection we might want the visible testimony of God's acceptance of His offering, the visible assurance that, as we had died in Him, the penalty of transgression was removed, and the power of death for ever broken. But surely, even without this visible testimony and assurance, we might have rested in the conclusion that a sacrifice so precious as that of Christ could not have been in vain. It might have delivered us, though it did not deliver Him, and we might have been called to everlasting gratitude towards One who gave Himself for us, and who died that we might live. Christ's Resurrection need not have been necessary to set us free from the punishment of those sins which He bore in His own body on the cross; and to tell us, therefore, that if Christ be not raised we are yet in our sins, because He is yet in our sins, is to use language which is either difficult to understand, or which, if we do understand it, is at variance with the reason of the case.

The truth is, that the whole question has been perplexed by the tendency alike of theologians and religious men to resolve Christ's work almost wholly if not wholly, into a plan of procuring pardon for the sinner, to view it too exclusively in its relation to the penalties of law, and to make holiness a consequence rather than an integral part of salvation. Such is not the Scripture method of looking at the matter. It is true that pardon has to be secured, that a violated law has to be satisfied, and that love, in return for the great love wherewith we have first been loved, has to be awakened in the Christian's breast, leading him into all cheerful obedience and all devout submission to his heavenly Father's will. Yet in the minds of the sacred writers there is something higher than any verdict of forgiveness that may be pronounced upon us, more important than our acquittal at the bar of God, more essentially, more intimately a part of our redeemed condition than gratitude, however lively, or love, however warm. There is that aspect of salvation which consists in life, life with Him and in Him who made us for Himself, the life of God in our souls, so that we shall be created again in the likeness of One in whose image we were originally made, and in conformity to whom the idea of our nature lies.

It was for this that the Lord Jesus Christ came. He came not to die, but to live; to submit indeed, in the first place, to death, because, as our Representative, He had to conform Himself to the great law everywhere prevailing in a sinful world, that death freely accepted is the only path to life; but then, having submitted to this, He came to rise to that life of perfect freedom which belongs to unreserved submission to the Father, and to yield Himself joyfully and for ever to the Father's service, as One who had fulfilled the commandment of the Father's love. To this life, too, He brings His people. They were with Him in His death; they are with Him in His life.

And now we see the connexion between the premiss and the conclusion of the Apostle's statement, that if Christ be not raised we are yet in our sins. We are yet in our natural condition, under the penalty, but especially under the power, of sin. Only in a Saviour who threw our sins off, and who rose to a life separated from all connexion with sin, can we throw our sins off, and rise to the higher, the heavenly, life. Only if Christ now lives the life of God can we live the life of God, for it is in Christ we live. If, therefore, Christ has not been raised, and is not now living with the Father, the very end of salvation must be left unanswered in us; our faith is vain; we are yet in our sins.

2. A second consequence that should make the Corinthian Christians careful how they accepted as an escape from difficulties the idea that Christ had not been raised, is contained in the 15th verse, "Yea, and we are found false witnesses of God; because we witnessed of God that He raised up Christ; whom He raised not up if so be that the dead are not raised up." The point is simple, and it needs little illustration. But it must have gone home with peculiar power to those to whom it was first presented. They knew in a manner of which we can probably form only a faint idea what the "witness" of St. Paul and of his fellow-Apostles meant. They had seen them in their labours and their sufferings, as they went from country to country and from city to city upon the great mission which they had undertaken. They had seen them abandon all the comforts of kindred and of home in order to devote themselves to a work in which they were exposed to contempt and scorn and persecution. What a life was that which the messengers of Christ then led! In this very Epistle St. Paul describes not only his own experience, but that of every other preacher of the cross in these days, when he says, "For I think that God hath set forth us the Apostles last of all, as it were doomed to death; for we are made a spectacle unto the world, both to angels and to men.

Even unto this present hour we both hunger, and thirst, and are naked, and are buffeted, and have no certain dwelling-place: we toil, we are reviled, we are persecuted, we are defamed, we are made as the filth of the world, the offscouring of all things even until now" (1 Cor. iv. 9-13); and in many another passage of his writings he lets us see how truly the words of his Divine Master had been fulfilled in His servants, "If they have persecuted me they will also persecute you."

What then was all this for? The answer was at hand. It was that they might witness to the death and Resurrection of Christ, that they might testify to what they had seen with their eyes, and heard with their ears, and their hands had handled of the word of life. Nor did they do this only of their own accord, urged on by natural impulses, or feeling themselves responsible to man alone. In this respect the words of ver. 15, "And we are found false witnesses of God," are peculiarly instructive, for they prove two things. First, St. Paul and those associated with him acted under the conviction that they witnessed not at the bar of man, but at the bar of the great Searcher of hearts and the great Judge of all. It was in the presence of God Himself that they spoke. The Divine eye was upon them; the Divine judgment was before them. They stood in the Divine presence, and not in the presence of any human tribunal, however great. Secondly, the very thought of falsehood in giving testimony in such circumstances could not be for a moment entertained. Such is the force of the words "we are found," which, according to New Testament usage, are by no means equivalent to "we are." They express what, in a real result, is its entire unexpectedness, its strange and inexplicable character; and they therefore lead us to think of that result as one, the existence of which it is hardly possible to conceive. Could then, is the argument, St. Paul and all those who witnessed with him have deliberately fabricated the story which they had proclaimed, or could they have had any intention to deceive? The thing was incredible. There are laws of human nature as true, and as certain in their operation, as the laws of the physical universe around us. You cannot believe, St. Paul would say, in the infraction of the one; can you believe in the infraction of the other? You will not believe that the dead shall be raised; can you believe that we, the living, are insensible to human motives, human aims, human fears, and human hopes? You know what we, who have borne witness, are; and to bring us in as false witnesses of God, when we say that Jesus was raised and is now alive in glory, is to involve yourselves in a contradiction from which a moment's reflection will show you that you have no escape.

3. A third consequence, intended to press home upon the Corinthian Christians the disastrous results that would flow from the fact, if it were true, that Christ had not been raised from the dead, is contained

in the 18th verse: " Then they also which are fallen asleep in Christ perished." The Authorized Version translates " are perished," the Revised Version " have perished." Neither translation conveys the force of the original. The Apostle does not merely say that the persons of whom he speaks are now in a state to which the word " perished " may be applied, but that *at the moment when they died* they perished. He takes his readers back to the solemn hour when they had been called upon to part with the Christian friends whom they had loved. Had these died the martyr's death, as he himself had seen Stephen die, then what was the meaning of that steadfast looking up into heaven, of that sight of the glory of God and Jesus standing on the right hand of God, or of the words, "Lord Jesus, receive my spirit," "Lord, lay not this sin to their charge," after which the martyr " fell asleep " ? Was it all a delusion ?. Was there no victory there ? no rest at last found in Him for whom the martyr suffered ? Or, had they died in their own beds, he then asks his readers to enter with him again into that chamber of death which had left such indelible traces on their memories. He recalls the circumstances of a scene which they remembered with a tenderness of feeling unequalled by that of any other through which they had passed. He bids them look again into the countenance worn with sickness yet full of hope, into the eyes closing on this world but already lighting up with the beams that came from another and a better,—and he says, as it were, to them, You remember these things, these hours in the history of honoured and beloved friends who had lived in Christ, and were now dying as they had lived. You then resigned them into the hands of a Redeemer who had lain in the grave before them, who had been raised from the grave, and who was waiting for them on the other side of the dark waters of death. You said to them, as the last sigh was about to escape from their lips, We shall meet again; and from that hour to this you have consoled yourselves with the reflection that they sleep in Christ, their souls with Him, their bodies resting in the grave till the resurrection. Has all this been a delusion? Instead of this did they "perish," forsaken of God, and separated from Him whom they had loved and served? It cannot be. Yet so it must be if Christ has not been raised. There is no other hope.

The appeal is made to the deepest instincts of our nature. It is not a proof, and it is not intended to be a proof, either that Christ has risen or that we shall rise. It is an appeal to feeling, a statement of the disastrous consequences that will follow from our denying that Resurrection of Christ with which the resurrection of His people is inseparably connected. We cannot believe that the good of all past generations, that those who, even amidst the frailties of the flesh, were yet distinguished by so much that was pure and noble and beautiful, that those who had wound themselves about our hearts, not only by the ties of natural affection, but by secret charms of character, hidden it may be from the world, but known in the privacy of the family and the home, have perished without the hope of ever being united either to Him or to us who know that we, with them, have been made partakers of His eternal life. Was God their Father? Was there such a thing as a fatherly relation between Him and them? Can we explain their existence as they were without supposing them to be His children? And did He so train them by His providence and grace that, long before the instant of their falling asleep, they were "in Christ," in the Holy One and the Just, who was day by day fashioning them into a greater likeness with Himself? How then, if they have perished, shall we resist the darkest views of Pessimism?

> Count o'er the joys thine eyes have seen,
> Count o'er thy days from anguish free,
> And know, whatever thou hast been,
> 'Tis something better not to be.

4. A fourth and last consideration, intended to bring home to his readers, not the fact, but the vast importance of the fact, that Christ is living still, is contained in the 19th verse: "If in this life only we have hoped in Christ, we are of all men most pitiable." The marginal rendering of the Revised Version is to be preferred: "If we have only hoped in Christ in this life, we are of all men most pitiable;" and the meaning is, that if our hope in Christ comes to an end with this present life, if it does not carry us

on to another and a better world, where we shall be reunited to Him and shall live with Him for ever, then are we far more deserving of pity than other men.

The words are difficult, and have often given rise to misapprehension. Let us observe (1) that St. Paul is not dealing with the supposition that, apart from the resurrection, the soul may live on after death separated from the body. It may be said that the resurrection is not necessary to our future welfare; that if the soul be saved it is enough; and that, if at death the spirit of man returns to the Father of Spirits, it may then continue to exist in the possession of such a purely spiritual joy that it shall not miss a human frame, but shall rather be like an imprisoned bird let loose to rise and float in its native element. Such thoughts, it would seem, are strange to the Apostle and to Scripture generally. At all events they are not here. St. Paul thinks of man as he knew him, in his compound personality of both body and spirit; and it is enough for him, therefore, to contemplate the possibility of man's not reaching as a whole eternal happiness. (2) The Apostle does not discuss the question whether virtue and goodness are not in themselves a great reward. Let us suppose a case put to him—the case of a man who, without thought of God, the sanctions of religion, or the expectation of a future life, devotes himself to the love and practice of whatever is most estimable and good. Let such an one do his utmost to expel sin from his heart, to train his own character, to benefit his fellow-creatures, to encourage every benevolent enterprise, to exhibit generosity and tenderness of heart; and then let us ask the Apostle whether that man has no reward in his goodness alone? He would surely not have answered in the negative. He who proclaimed to his heathen hearers at Athens a God in whom all men live and move and have their being; who recognised the craving of the human heart, apart from direct Christian instruction, after an invisible and supreme Ruler of the universe; who exhorted the Philippians to the practice of whatever things were true and honourable, and just and pure, and lovely and of good report, and who even spoke of creation itself as groaning and travailing in pain along with man; he, in short, who shows in all his writings how much he values the principles of natural as well as revealed religion, could never have said that a virtuous life in the commonest acceptation of the term would in itself, and apart from the hope of immortality, have made men "pitiable." No one would have allowed more fully that virtue must bring with it its own reward, and that even for its own sake it was worthy to be pursued.

What then does St. Paul really mean by the language of this 19th verse? We shall understand him better if we attend to the following considerations:—

(1.) The word he uses is not "miserable," but "pitiable" ($\dot{\epsilon}\lambda\epsilon\epsilon\iota\nu\acute{o}\varsigma$). He does not say that in this life Christians are "miserable," because in fighting the good fight of faith and running the Christian race they have to take up their cross and suffer, as if virtue would not be worth suffering for, even although there should be no happy future in store. What he says is, that they of whom he speaks are of all men "most pitiable," that there are none whose life is so built upon sand that will be at once swept away beneath them when the great trial comes, none the very essence and aim and animating principle of whose being will one day be proved to have been so utterly deceptive.

(2.) For, observe the difference between the naturally righteous man and the man righteous in the power of Christian faith, the difference which marks the principle and regulates the extent of their respective righteousnesses. Both, the Apostle would have said, are what they are in Christ in whom "were all things created" (Col. i. 16); but the latter alone knows and sees this, and is alone alive to the fact that he lives, not by One who framed the fabric of the universe and of man at the beginning, but in One who is even now a living Lord at the right hand of the Father, sending down His quickening, living, eternal Spirit into all the members of His Body to make them like Himself the Head.

(3.) If, therefore, there be no Risen, glorified Christ, which of the two has been living most in dreams of the night, in fantastic imaginations of the brain? Not the former. He thought of this world alone, and he had his reward. But surely the latter, all the most powerful motives of whose life are shown to have rested on a delusion, and who has never grasped anything but a shadow. We "pity" him not because it is not worth while to live or even die for what is good, or as if the joy of goodness cannot repay suffering for its sake, but because it is always sad to see men spending time and strength upon what must prove at last to have had no reality, and because the sadness deepens in proportion to the loftiness of the expectation that is dashed to the ground.

(4.) All this is confirmed when we remember that the deepest element of the Christian life is suffering, is, in one sense or another, cross-bearing. The cross of Christ was not simply a temporary incident in the life of Jesus. It is an eternal principle in His kingdom. All His disciples must take up their cross and follow Him if they would really be partakers of His Spirit; and why should they do so, when they might, at least to a large extent, avoid it, unless they believe that, like their Master, both they themselves and those for whom they suffer have the rewards of another and a higher life in view? Self-denial and self-sacrifice are virtues that spring from a higher order of things than that of time, and if Christ be not raised up and glorified we shall seek in vain for such an order to be either our guide or strength.

Thus then does the Apostle enforce the arguments which he had used against those Christians at Corinth who denied the resurrection of the dead. His appeal has been to fact and to fact alone. His reasoning on the subject, the light that he is to cast upon the fact when it has its place assigned to it in God's eternal and universal plan, is still to come. In the meantime his one cry has been, Behold the fact, Christ is risen. He could not have risen if dead men rise not; and if He be not risen, the oracles of God's grace which satisfy the aspirations of man as he presses on to the perfection for which he longs may be for ever dumb; the deepest principles of human nature are overthrown; the tenderest and most sacred affections of our hearts are crushed; and life itself, with all that most ennobles and beautifies it, becomes a burden and a sorrow.

"But now hath Christ been raised from the dead, the first-fruits of them that are asleep. For since by man came death, by man came also the resurrection of the dead. For as in Adam all die, so also in Christ shall all be made alive."—1 COR. xv. 20-22. [R.V.]

Chapter iii.

THE words "But now" with which the Apostle begins ver. 20 are not the mere expression of time. In a sense in which we frequently meet them in his writings, they are used to denote the whole circumstances of the case, the change that had passed upon the old order of things, and the new order that had been introduced: "But now, apart from the law, a righteousness of God hath been manifested." "But now hath God set the members each one of them in the body, even as it pleased Him." "But now abideth faith, hope, love, these three" (Rom. iii. 21 ; 1 Cor. xii. 18, xiii. 13). At the point, therefore, of the Apostle's argument that we have reached, he evidently throws off, as with a shout of joy and triumph, the miserable consequences which he had shown in the immediately preceding verses must inevitably flow from an admission of the idea that Christ had not been raised from the dead. Christian preaching was not, as it would then have been, the proclamation of a meaningless and empty message. Christian faith was not a principle incapable of producing any good results. The Apostles and messengers of the Lord were not false witnesses daring, under the very eye of God and in the light of His coming judgment, to announce as a fact what they knew was not a fact. The Christian dead had not perished, but were still under the guardianship of a Risen and Living Lord ; and Christians still alive, instead of being of all men most pitiable because resting their whole life on a delusion, and continually sacrificing what the voice of nature bade them keep, were rather of all men most blessed. Their hope was sure, an anchor of the soul ; and the light afflictions of this life, which were only for a moment, were not worthy to be compared with the glory that should be revealed to them. All was safe then : all was bright and full of glad expectation. Christ was risen, and His people shall also rise.

But the great thought which filled the Apostle's mind was one that needed further expansion and illustration. Christ actually raised from the dead! Dead men actually to rise! There was something in the contemplation of such an idea that could not fail to startle, and to rouse incredulity to the very uttermost. It may seem to us easy to accept the statement. It is only easy when we occupy ourselves with words instead of things. The moment we realize what it means, difficulties spring up on every side ; and we are compelled to ask, not for external proof only of what appears to be so singular and isolated a fact, but for internal demonstration of its reasonableness, of its adaptation to the nature

CHAP. III   THE RESURRECTION OF THE DEAD   43

of man, and of its harmony with all the other dealings of the Almighty in a universe which, if it has a supreme Creator and Governor, must be one consistent whole. To answer such questions, and to throw light upon such a mystery, is what St. Paul has now before him.

1. First, he re-states the facts in another form with which his Christian readers were familiar: " But now hath Christ been raised from the dead, the first-fruits (the words " and become " of the Authorized Version are to be omitted) of them that are asleep."

The figure is taken from the beautiful ceremony of the Law described in Lev. xxiii. 10-12: " When ye be come into the land which I give unto you, and shall reap the harvest thereof, then ye shall bring the sheaf of the first-fruits of your harvest; and ye shall wave the sheaf before the Lord, to be accepted for you: on the morrow after the Sabbath the priest shall wave it. And in the day when ye wave the sheaf, ye shall offer a he-lamb without blemish of the first year for a burnt-offering unto the Lord." That is, at the season of the Passover, when the barley harvest, the earliest harvest of the year, was beginning to ripen, a sheaf of ripe ears (for so the injunction was understood) was to be gathered from the fields near Jerusalem, and was to be waved in solemn dedication to the Lord. The day chosen for the ceremonial was that following the Sabbath, or, in other words, our Sunday, the first day of the week, which came after the celebration of the Paschal Feast. That sheaf was not dedicated to God merely because it was the earliest ripened. It had a symbolic meaning. It was the first-fruits of the harvest of the whole congregation, and it signified that the entire harvest of the year was God's. It was a pledge and earnest that every sheaf of the season would be regarded in the same sacred light alike by God and Israel. All the sheaves of the year were lifted up in thought out of their natural condition; and though all, with the one single exception, were given to the people for food, they followed the first in the essential notion of their elevated and consecrated character. The binding nature of the tie between the first-fruits and the remainder of the harvest, and the dedication of all to God, still further symbolized by the burnt-offering of the lamb, is thus the leading feature of the ceremonial here referred to.

This figure then is now used by the Apostle, and we cannot fail to see that it is used with peculiar appropriateness when we remember that it was on the first day of the week, on the Sunday after our Passover was sacrificed for us, that the Lord Jesus rose. On that morning He, the first sheaf of the ripening corn, was presented to His Father in His risen and glorified condition, that not as a single individual only, but as including in Himself the harvest to follow, He might thenceforward, through obedience and submission to the

Father's will, be a continual burnt-offering, sending up the savour of a sweet smell in the heavenly sanctuary.

Such is the figure; and, looked at with eyes well acquainted with the rites of Israel, it helped, even alone, to prepare the way for what was to follow. If Christ rose as the first-fruits of them that are asleep, they can no more be separated from Him than the body of the harvest from the first sheaf of it that was waved before the Lord.

2. Secondly, still deeper thoughts, however, are in the Apostle's mind, and to them he proceeds in the two next following verses: "For since by man came death, by man came also the resurrection of the dead. For as in the Adam all die, so in the Christ shall all be made alive" (vers. 21, 22).

Before speaking of the principle involved in these verses, it may be well to examine the extent of that effect which is ascribed to it, or, in other words, the meaning of the clause, "all shall be made alive." At first sight it may seem as if we ought to adopt what is generally a safe rule of interpretation, and to understand this clause in the sense which it most easily and naturally bears. But such a rule obviously implies that the words under consideration shall not be wrested from their context, or be considered apart from the whole thought that is at the moment in the writer's mind. To ascertain that thought is the aim of the interpreter; and if he is successful in doing so, he is in possession of a test by which he is not only entitled, but bound to try any meaning, however easy and natural, which belongs to a portion of the argument, and if necessary to reject it. In the present instance the application of this rule is at once fatal to the literal acceptation of the words before us. The verb ζωοποιηθήσονται (" shall be made alive ") cannot mean simply " shall be raised from the grave." It will admit of but one interpretation, " shall be made alive with spiritual and eternal life." Not only its connexion with ζωή, but the fact that it bears this signification in every passage in which, when applied to persons, it occurs in the New Testament (John v. 21, vi. 63; Rom. iv. 17, viii. 11; 1 Cor. xv. 45; 2 Cor. iii. 6; Gal. iii. 21), is conclusive upon the point. If, therefore, we interpret the word " all " literally, in its sense of universality, the Apostle must be understood to say that all men, without exception, having died in " the Adam " shall be saved with the full Messianic salvation in " the Christ." The statement made will and can only be, a statement of redemption in its most unlimited and most unrestricted form—in a form so unrestricted that universalists themselves cannot accept it. Even they do not urge that persons who have died or, it may be, lived on to the very hour of the Redeemer's Coming, in determined rebellion against God, shall at once pass into the full enjoyment of a heavenly life. Such a conception they would acknowledge to be impossible; and they would plead for no more than this, that at some point in a distant eternity, and after whatever discipline may be thought necessary by the Almighty, every wanderer shall be reclaimed, and every trace of sin extinguished in the reign of unmingled and triumphant good. We know too that, in other passages of his writings, St. Paul has given the clearest expression possible to the truth, that the judgment which brings eternal life to some, brings wrath and indignation, tribulation and anguish, to others (Rom. ii. 6-11; 2 Thess. i. 6-10). The plainest rules, therefore, of grammatical and historical interpretation forbid us to understand the words before us in that meaning which may at first sight strike us as simplest and most natural.

A second interpretation is proposed. The statement of the Apostle, it is said, may mean that while all die in Adam, the possibility of salvation is in Christ within the reach of every man. Salvation may not be universal in its *application*, but, it is so in its *offer*. If any one is not saved, the fault lies with himself, and neither with Christ nor with the Gospel. The Redeemer of the world, with all His benefits, is brought within the reach, and is urged upon the acceptance, of every fallen child of Adam. This interpretation may satisfy for a moment, but not long. The contrast, the antithesis, between the two clauses before us is too marked to permit our resting in it as a full explanation of the words. In the Adam all died; in the Christ all shall be made alive. Nothing can be more direct or more explicit than the language. In the one case death is not merely threatened, but inflicted. To say that in the other life is simply offered, can be regarded as little less than an evasion of the difficulty.

A third interpretation has been recently offered to which it seems desirable to allude. The statement of St. Paul is supposed to rest upon the fact that we are not only redeemed, but created, in Christ; that through Him there is in every man a principle of good as well as evil; or, as it might be expressed in the language of St. John, that there is a "true light which lighteth every man that cometh into the world" (chap. i. 9). This light is then thought to be kindled in us through the *redemptive* work of Christ, which so stretches back in its efficacy that in the original conception of our nature we are made partakers of its benefits. By virtue of it we were not only redeemed, we were made as we are, and from the very beginning, side by side with the human and imperfect nature which we inherit in Adam, lie the elements of the divine and perfect nature which we inherit in Christ. "Even before we believe, we have two natures, two men, in us; or, as we phrase it, we have a better and a worse self contending in us for the mastery." Thus the redeeming work of Christ, going back to the instant when our first parents were created is not less extensive, while it is at the same time richer, deeper, and fuller in its effects than was the Fall.[1] "As

[1] Cox, *The Resurrection*, chap. iii.

in Adam all die, so also in Christ shall all be made alive."

It may be at once allowed that this explanation has both an interest of its own in relation to the present passage, and that it connects itself with an important lesson of the Word of God,—that the redemption given us in our Lord is not an afterthought of the Divine mind, but something lying in the original conception of man and of man's destiny. Yet it does not resolve the difficulties with which we have at present to contend. For, in the first place, the death which men are here said to die in Adam is not a mere principle of evil to be contended with and overcome. It includes physical death, that lying down in the grave from which those with whom St. Paul is arguing declared there was no resurrection. It includes therefore what cannot be escaped, what comes upon all men whether they will or no. In the second place, the "life" here spoken of is no victory gained in this present world, which, too, unless kept steadfast hold of, may again be lost. It is the life of the future world, *begun in the resurrection from the grave*; and which, when it has been once obtained, can never be lost. In the third place, the words "shall be made alive" take our thoughts distinctly to the future as the time when the gift shall be bestowed, and not to the past as a time when it was bestowed long ago. Whatever interest, therefore, may attach to this view, the laws of legitimate interpretation are against it.

In these circumstances there is really no alternative but to ask whether that is not a well-grounded interpretation which sees in the Apostle's words a contrast between two different lines of descent, the one from Adam, the other from Christ; and whether the "all" spoken of in the second clause may not refer to those alone who have embraced Christ in faith and are now in Him. Not a little in the passage seems to justify such a conclusion.

For (1) it is impossible to separate the use of the words "them that are asleep" (τῶν κεκοιμημένων) in ver. 20 from the words "that are fallen asleep" (κοιμηθέντες) in ver. 18; and, connected as the word is in the latter verse with the additional words "in Christ," no one can imagine that there at least others than true believers are referred to. (2) The word "firstfruits" of ver. 20 leads to the same conclusion. What the first-fruits are, the harvest is, the same in consecration, the same in glory; and the connexion between ver. 20 and ver. 21 leaves no doubt that in the clause "shall all be made alive" we have simply the harvest presented to us in another form. (3) The words "they that are Christ's" in ver. 23 express not less clearly the same class of persons as that embodied in the conception of the harvest, and equally show that St. Paul is thinking only of such as shall hereafter share the glory of their Lord at His coming. (4) The special force of the word "in" before the words "the Adam" and "the Christ" ought to be attended to. It seems to imply more than the mere fact that there is a connexion between two different sections of the human family and their respective heads, bringing with it in the one case death, in the other life. The expression "in Christ" is too common in the writings of St. Paul to permit us to rest in such a superficial view in the case of the second of the two clauses of which we speak; and if it possesses a deeper meaning there, it is probable that the same meaning may also be found in the first clause. In both, therefore, it would seem that the word "in" points to a connexion freely accepted and partaken of, a bond of will, a bond of consent on the part of a posterity which, in spirit, disposition, and character, adopts and approves of its likeness to its first progenitor.

There still remains, indeed, a certain difficulty arising from the fact that we thus appear to take the first "all" of ver. 22 in an unrestricted, the second in a restricted sense; and, to escape this difficulty, it has been proposed to confine that word to believers in the first as well as in the second case. Something may be said for this, especially when we observe that in ver. 24 there is a similar restriction in the use of the word. "All rule and all authority and power" cannot mean these things universally, but only such of them as are opposed to Christ. We may have a similar restriction here; and if we restrict to believers, as the only persons spoken of, the "all" who in Adam have death as well as the "all" who in Christ have life, we shall preserve the complete parallelism of the two. Whatever may be urged on behalf of this expedient, it is unnecessary to resort to it; nor does there appear to be any good reason why, with perfect fairness of interpretation, we should not understand the word "all" when it occurs the second time in an apparently more limited sense than that in which it is used the first time. It is really not more limited from *the particular point of view from which the Apostle treats his subject.* Whether in the second instance "all" be universal or not is not the main consideration in his argument. That it shall be equally extensive in both clauses is not his point. What he concerns himself about is, that there is such a bond of connexion between two different heads and their descendants that the latter partake of everything contained in the former. He beholds two great companies marshalled before his eye, possessed of entirely different characteristics, and involved in entirely different fates. On the one hand there is the whole human family, on the other are all who are raised in glory. Of those raised not in glory, but in shame, he does not for an instant think. There is not the slightest trace of them, as we shall afterwards have occasion to notice more fully, in the passage. He does not see them. They are as much out of his field of vision as if they were non-existent. He sees the two companies above mentioned, and them alone; and, looking at them, he describes the condition of "all" of the one as death in the Adam, that of "all" of the other as life in the Christ. We have only to work ourselves into the Apostle's method of isolating the thought with which he deals at any particular moment from every other, however related to it, in order to see that the two " alls " need not be absolutely co-extensive. They are equally co-extensive in the only light in which it concerns him at present to regard them.

By these considerations also we are at least guided towards the reply to be made to those who complain that, take the words before us in any sense whatever, the parallel is still incomplete. Our death, it is said, does not depend on our faith in Adam; and, as our life depends upon our faith in Christ, there is a want of perfect correspondence between the clauses thus brought together. The answer to this difficulty lies in the consideration of who "the Christ" is of whom the Apostle speaks. Let it be particularly noticed that he does not say "Christ," but "the Christ," a rendering which ought certainly to have stood in the text, not the margin, of the Revised Version. In ver. 20 he had used the expression "Christ" without the article, because there he is dealing with the personal Redeemer, of whom he says that He " hath been raised from the dead." In ver. 22 he changes the expression and speaks of "the Christ," because it is now necessary not to think only of the person, but of the work of the Redeemer, of His whole work, of all that is involved in Him. One of the most essential parts of this, however, is Christ's Resurrection from the grave, and the thought of that Resurrection is therefore part of the thought wrapped up in the words "the Christ." "The Christ," in short, of ver. 22 is the risen Christ. But Christ risen is, even while risen in the body, essentially "spirit." In this very chapter the raised up body is "a spiritual body" (ver. 44). How then can one be connected with "the Christ" except by a *spiritual* principle ? Want of completeness can be assigned to the parallel only when we fail to notice this true meaning of "the Christ." Were Christ only man the parallel would fail, and the Apostle might be charged with false reasoning. But the moment we keep in view that "the Christ" is the risen, the spiritual Christ—that moment we see that the physical bond of connexion in the one case *must* be responded to by the spiritual bond of faith in the other.

The Adam and the Christ then, the Adam who fell in Eden, the Christ who now reigns in glory, are the representatives of all who are found in them. It is the great principle of heredity, the principle by which, because they view it in an aspect too exclusively physical, while they neglect to balance it by its complementary principle of moral freedom, men in our day too often extinguish at one stroke the dignity of our nature, and reduce us to the level of plants or animals, each bearing seed in the likeness of its own kind. But the principle of heredity, viewed as it ought to be, is attended with no such consequences. It is rather a principle of the Almighty's well ordered government, not an arbitrary principle, not a principle brought in in the case of the believer, to put right what had gone wrong, but a fundamental principle, one necessary to the consolidation, the union, and the welfare of the race. We see it operating in every nation, class, and family of man. Troubled though it may be by the intrusion of many of our own motives of action, it is still there. Once, or rather twice, we see it clear at its starting-points in the Adam and the Christ, in the one conveying sin and death because of sin, in the other righteousness and life because of righteousness, to "all" who are in the Adam or in the Christ.

3. Thirdly, one other point in these verses remains to be examined, where St. Paul speaks of the root-principle out of which this arrangement springs: "For, since by man came death, by man came also the resurrection of the dead" (ver. 21). There is more here than the statement of a *fact* which the Apostle had observed. He is dealing with a fundamental and eternal *principle*, and he shows that he is doing so by his use of the word "since." As acknowledged by the best and most recent commentators (*e. g.* Edwards *in loc.*), that word is not the simple introduction to a parallelism. "It means," says Edwards, "much more than resemblance, and more than fitness or congruity. It expresses the necessity that there should be a new head of the race, and an organic centre of life. The necessity arises from our need of redemption. *Because* through one man sin came into the world, through union with a new source came redemption, and through

redemption life." This is undoubtedly the thought, but it needs to be unfolded. Why this necessity? Whence this *because*? The argument appears to be as follows. No man is a mere unit in creation. No man stands alone in the world, called into existence by a separate *fiat* of the Creator, unconnected with either the men who have gone before, or the men who are to come after him. He is part of an organism in which his being is transmitted to him, and in which he again transmits being to others. That is a part of his nature. Without it he would not be man. The descendant, too, corresponds to the progenitor. The latter does not transmit to the former something different from what he is. He may be said rather to transmit himself. Whatever the progenitor is, the descendant will in his turn be. Whatever the descendant is, the progenitor must have been. Was the progenitor flesh, the descendant will be flesh. Was the progenitor spirit, the descendant will be spirit; and the bond connecting the two must necessarily partake of the same characteristics. It must be fleshly in the one case, spiritual in the other. If, therefore, sinful men were to be brought to redemption and life, it was not simply necessary that there should be a new head, a new source, from which they were to spring. It was further necessary that, in effecting this, the line of continuity should be preserved, so that man might be treated as man, and might reach his destiny, not by an arbitrary bound, but along those lines which lie in the very constitution of his being, and lead to its full development. Had it been otherwise, his nature would not have been dealt with as it is. In the process of perfecting it, its most essential characteristics would have been changed. No longer as man, but as some other being altogether, would he have reached his goal.

Again, the attainment of this perfection implies victory over death. Inseparably connected with the thought of both sin and the weakness of the flesh, exhibiting in its ravages the fatal consequences of the one and the helplessness of the other, death is that in which all that now prevents man's perfection culminates; and it is overcome only by resurrection. Nothing less than resurrection is true victory over death. Even although man dies in peace; although he obeys without a murmur the call that summons him from a present world; although, before the last struggle begins, he has prevailed over that fear of death to which he has all along been subject, it cannot be said that by these things death is overcome. It is not "abolished," or brought to nought (ver. 26), by any mere triumph of faith. If nothing more can be said, there will still be one great sense in which death remains the conqueror in the final war, and the helplessness of the body from which life is fled will be the token of its spoils. Resurrection alone affords a complete victory over death.

Hence it is that the Apostle looks upon the "resurrection of the dead" as the necessary destiny of redeemed man; and, as "the Adam" cannot lead us to that destiny, for through him we inherit death, the Almighty has another and final mode by which it may be accomplished. As, too, it can only be accomplished in a manner corresponding to the nature of those who are to be redeemed, he who executes it must be truly human. In other words, "As by man came death, by man must come also the resurrection of the dead." One thing only has to be kept steadily in view. Throughout these verses the Apostle never takes his eye off the risen Christ. As "the first-fruits" of them that sleep Christ is risen. As the man by whom came the resurrection of the dead He is risen. As "the Christ" in contrast with "the Adam" He is risen. It is not from a Christ simply incarnate that the new humanity springs: it is from an incarnate Christ exalted and glorified. The latter alone transmits to us His spiritual, unchanging, everlasting life; and because, though still essentially man, He is spirit, it is only by a spiritual bond that we can be connected with, and united to, Him.

That union then has taken place. We believe,—and, as Christ has risen from the dead, as that is a part of His history not less certain than it is a part of the first Adam's history that he fell and died, the fruits of His victory shall certainly be made ours, because we are His. Sprung from the risen Saviour, who is spirit, in that line of spiritual descent which is the only possible one where spirit not flesh is concerned, Christians can have no doubt that the experience of the Head will, in due time, be that of the members. The Resurrection of their Lord brings theirs along with it. They are in the same bundle of life with Him; and, when He comes again, it will only be to receive them unto Himself, that where He is there they may be also.

"But each in his own order: Christ the first-fruits; then they that are Christ's, at his coming. Then cometh the end, when he shall deliver up the kingdom to God, even the Father; when he shall have abolished all rule and all authority and power. For he must reign, till he hath put all his enemies under his feet. The last enemy that shall be abolished is death. For, He put all things in subjection under his feet. But when he saith, All things are put in subjection, it is evident that he is excepted who did subject all things unto him. And when all things have been subjected unto him, then shall the Son also himself be subjected to him that did subject all things unto him, that God may be all in all."—1 COR. xv. 23-28. [R.V.]

Chapter iv.

WITH the close of 1 Cor. xv. 22 the Apostle had really accomplished the end which he had in view in this chapter, for he had shown that, as Christ was raised up from the dead, His people shall also in due time be raised up. The scepticism at Corinth, which found expression in the words, "There is no resurrection of the dead," had been met and answered. In God's great plan there was not only an original head of the whole human race; a second head of a new development in that race had appeared. All the members, both of the race and of the new development, were the direct descendants of their respective heads, were connected with them by an appropriate bond, and inherited what each head, according to an unchangeable principle of the Divine government, transmitted to its posterity. These two heads were Adam and the risen and glorified Redeemer. Both had the nature of man, so that their descendants were human. Both, as the law of heredity required, transmitted their life, their blood, themselves, so that in each child of Adam there was a true sense in which we see Adam, in each child of Christ, a sense not less true in which we see Christ. At each point of the one line, therefore, we behold a human being under that law of sin and death to which Adam by his fall was made subject; at each point of the other line we behold a human being under that law of perfect righteousness and everlasting life which marks Him who, having died once, dieth no more, but dwells for ever in the Father's presence and in the enjoyment of His glory. Finally, the bond connecting each member of the two lines of descent was appropriate to the nature alike of the head and of the members. As the one head was flesh, the bond was in that case fleshly; as the other head was spirit, the bond was in that case spiritual. These bonds were perfectly distinct. Each led only to its own natural result,— flesh to sin and that death which is the wages of sin, spirit to righteousness and that life beyond the grave which is the victory over death. No one simply under the influence of either bond alone could have an interest in what was associated exclusively with the other. He who had no position except that belonging to the first line could not share in what was transmitted through the second head. Could any instance be produced of one standing only in the second line, he would have no share in what is transmitted through the first head. All these thoughts, though they may not be fully worked out in vers. 20-22, are clearly in the mind of the Apostle; and, if we do not admit that they are so, it will not only be impossible to see the force of his reasoning, it will even be difficult to see that his reasoning is logically correct.

One remark further may be made in passing. What has been said at once convicts of incorrectness that method of theological statement which represents our Lord as the Head of a new humanity in which *all* men, whether they are or are not in possession of the spiritual bond with Him that has been spoken of, mystically share. Christ *is* the head of a new humanity to those alone who are brought by " spirit " into that line of descent which springs from Him. He is not the Head of a new humanity to those who, disowning and rejecting the influence of " spirit," refuse the only bond by which that new humanity can be made theirs. The language to which we object is therefore, to say the least, ambiguous. But it appears to be, at the same time, on the part of those who most frequently employ it, a mistake, for it flows from the idea that Christ, as incarnate, is the Head of the new humanity, whereas the whole teaching of St. Paul rests on the conception that that Head is to be found in the Christ who is not only incarnate, but is risen, exalted, and glorified. It is not easy to say how much this latter truth, restored to its proper place, would affect our systems of theology.

But to return. Although the Apostle has gained the point which he had chiefly in view, he cannot dismiss the subject. It rises before him far too great in its interest, far too grave in the particulars belonging to it, to be thus hastily set aside. We long to hear more, and he has more to tell. He accordingly proceeds to describe more fully the manner in which the plan of the resurrection is carried out, including in one brief summary the whole chain of events connected with it from its beginning to its close. This also he seems to do in such a way as to show that the whole is a well-ordered plan, suitable to Him who is the ultimate centre of all existence, who has established the harmony of the universe, and the promotion of whose glory must be the issue to which all things tend.

At ver. 23 he goes on, "But each in his own order: Christ the first-fruits; then they that are Christ's at His presence. Then *cometh* the end, when He shall deliver up the kingdom to God, even the Father; when He shall have brought to nought all rule and all authority and power. For He must reign till He hath put all His enemies under His feet. The last enemy that shall be abolished is death. For, He put all things in subjection under His feet."

It is unnecessary to dwell upon the word "order," upon the ranks or sections which, in the process spoken of, pass before our view. Of these there appear to be only two: first, Christ Himself; secondly, the army of the redeemed. Thus it was in the barley-harvest. Of its parts also we may say, "Each in its own order:" first, the sheaf of the first-fruits; secondly, the remaining harvest of the year. Many indeed urge that we have here a distinct intimation of three ranks of the resurrection army: first, Christ Himself; secondly, the righteous who have fallen asleep in Him; thirdly, after an interval of the length of which no mention is made, the wicked, whose raising up is to be immediately followed by the general judgment. Of those who take this view of the passage, Pfleiderer may be quoted as the most recent and able representative. "In ver. 23," he says, "the order (τάγμα) of the resurrection is discussed: first of all is Christ 'the first-fruits;' *then* at His παρουσία follow those who are Christ's;—εἶτα τὸ τέλος, *i.e.* then is the end of the resurrection, namely, the resurrection of all, which moment will be at the same time the end of all things, the end of this present world-period, because it coincides in time with the giving over of the sovereignty to God (ὅταν παραδιδῷ τὴν βασιλείαν τῷ θεῷ, *sc.* ὁ Χριστός—note the present tense παραδιδῷ, which indicates that this giving over is simultaneous with the end of the resurrection). We therefore have here a series of moments of the resurrection, in which each is separated in time from the preceding one; this is expressed by ἀπαρχή — ἔπειτα — εἶτα. This distinct idea of a τάγμα, which consists of different parts, and comprises different periods of time, would be altogether destroyed by supposing that εἶτα τὸ τέλος is simultaneous with the preceding ἔπειτα . . . παρουσίᾳ αὐτοῦ; for in that case there would be, at the coming of Christ, only *one thing*, namely, the resurrection of the Christians, to be expected besides that of Christ, which had preceded it, which evidently would give no ground for speaking of a 'series;' and, moreover, the fate of the entire non-Christian world would have been passed over in silence in an inconceivable manner."[1] Pfleiderer thus interposes a long period between the παρουσία and the τέλος, that period being occupied with Christ's visible exercise of the sovereignty which He had until that time exercised invisibly through the Spirit, and being terminated by the resurrection of the wicked and the general judgment. At the παρουσία Christ *enters upon* this visible authority, this visible contending with and conquering of all hostile powers: at the τέλος Christ *gives up* this His βασιλεία to the Father, and God is all in all: the interval is the Millennium of the Apocalypse, though St. Paul says nothing of its duration being limited to a thousand years. At the same time, Pfleiderer frankly admits not only that the internal character of this Pauline Millennium differs from that of the Johannine, but that the whole conception of it is inconsistent with St. Paul's teaching elsewhere, and is a proof that the Apostle had not yet been able to shake off the remnants of his Jewish theology, although he had failed to harmonize it with his advanced Christian γνῶσις. The point is thus of much greater importance than may at first be supposed, and it deserves careful consideration.

[1] *Paulinism*, translated by Peters, vol. i. p. 268.

1. The idea of St. Paul's inconsistency with himself may be speedily dismissed. Were such inconsistency established, the true inference would be that one or other of the documents, the statements of which could not be brought to tally with each other, was not the genuine production of the Apostle. In the present case it is impossible to urge this, for the other document mainly referred to is the Epistle to the Romans, and no one doubts that both it and 1 Corinthians proceeded from St. Paul's pen. That there should be inconsistency between these two great Epistles, written with but a short interval of time between them, upon a question of such deep interest and importance as the winding up of the world's history, is a thought which no reasonable interpreter can for a moment entertain. Apparent inconsistency would simply prove that, in one or other of the places where the subject is referred to, we misunderstand the words.

2. The allegation that the mere existence of two terms is not sufficient to justify the Apostle in speaking of a "series" may be dismissed with equal ease. The word τάγμα involves in it no idea of a *lengthened* series. It probably denotes one's place in a series; and there may in this respect be such a difference between the position of two parties, not less than of three or four, as fully to justify its use. In the case of the first sheaf of the barley-harvest and of the harvest following it we have already had in ver. 20 a series of two. Each of these had its

own τάγμα. A similar illustration, when the word is employed in a military sense, is afforded by the thought of a captain and his company.

3. Almost as quickly we may dispose of the assertion that the Apostle's silence as to the fate of the non-Christian world is "inconceivable." If so, all the statements of the chapter are equally inconceivable, for it is throughout silent upon this point. From its first verse to its last it speaks of Christians and of Christians alone. Not only so. In 1 Thess. iv. 13-18, at a time when St. Paul is treating of the very subject that he has here before him, the resurrection of the dead, we have a precisely similar omission of all reference to non-Christians. In vers. 16 and 17 of that chapter, it seems at first sight to be the Apostle's intention to set forth all the events of the great day; and, if he does set them all forth, it would be a just inference that there is no resurrection for the wicked. But the explanation there is the same as here. The Apostle concerns himself only about the one thought with which he is dealing at the time.

4. As to the comparison with St. John in the Apocalypse, it is in the first place needless to say much, since Pfleiderer takes little interest in the measure of agreement which he himself allows, the measure of difference noted by him being much greater. And in the second place it is impossible in this paper to say much, for the real agreement between the two Apostles can only be brought out

by an argument far too long and intricate for the present discussion.[1]

5. The argument of Pfleiderer and those who agree with him breaks down on the fact, that they give a wholly false interpretation to the βασιλεία and the βασιλεύειν of Christ spoken of in vers. 24 and 25. They understand these words in the sense of the glory, honour, and happiness which belong to a royal reign, whereas the thought most prominent in them is that of royal *power*, and especially power for the destruction of enemies. The Apostle thinks of the reign of Ps. xlv.: "I speak of the things which I have made touching the King. . . . Thine arrows are sharp in the hearts of the King's enemies, whereby the people fall under Thee" (vers. 1, 5), or of Ps. cx.: "Rule Thou in the midst of Thine enemies. The Lord at Thy right hand shall strike through kings in the day of His wrath. He shall judge among the nations, He shall fill the places with dead bodies; He shall strike through the head in many countries" (vers. 2, 5, 6). That this is the light in which St. Paul looks at the "reign" of Christ is clear from his own language in vers. 24 and 25. In the first of these he says that Christ shall deliver up the kingdom "when He shall have *abolished* all rule and all authority and power;" in the second, that he must reign "till He hath put all His *enemies* under His feet;" and the first statement implies

---

[1] The writer may be permitted to refer for remarks bearing upon this point to his work, *Discussions on the Apocalypse*, v.

that the "kingdom" consists in "abolishing" what is spoken of, the second that the "reign" is occupied with "putting down" all the enemies of the King. There is not the slightest foundation, therefore, for the supposition that St. Paul teaches that there shall be a long reign of glory between the raising of believers and the "end," and that there is thus a third τάγμα introduced by εἶτα in ver. 24. The raising of believers is contemporaneous with the "end," and the Apostle has only two "orders" in his eye—Christ Himself at His Resurrection, and His people at theirs.

One other remark may be made.

6. Strangely enough, the idea of a threefold τάγμα in another form appears to be introduced by Edwards in his exposition of ver. 26, after his exposition of the previous verses leaves no room for it. He supposes that death has not been destroyed at the Second Coming, and at the resurrection of those that are Christ's. There are "two resurrections, the former of believers only, the latter of all others," and the teaching is regarded as similar to that of St. John in Rev. xx. with regard to the resurrections apparently separated from each other by a thousand years. But if, as allowed by this commentator, the resurrection of believers be coincident with the τέλος, and with the giving up of the mediatorial kingdom to God, the interval of time thus thought of becomes wholly unintelligible. We can attach no idea to what is meant by a resurrection

of the wicked a thousand years (or whatever the number may be) after the τέλος. Again, when it is said in ver. 25, "He hath put *all* His enemies under His feet," surely death must be included in the "all," especially when we have been already told at ver. 24 that the delivering up of the kingdom was then come. Had ver. 25 been designed to introduce a correction of that statement, it would have been necessary to do it in a much more definite manner. Again, it may be asked how the *resurrection of the wicked* can be the incident which of all others shows that the moment for the abolishing of death has arrived. It is, on the contrary, inconsistent with St. Paul's general treatment of the subject to think that he could have looked upon the former of these events as either a proof or an illustration of the latter. The truth is that there is no ground for interposing any period of time between vers. 24, 25, and ver. 26, "Death" in the latter verse is simply a part of the "*all* rule," etc., and of the "*all* His enemies" of the former verses; and it is selected out of the "all," having a distinct place assigned to it, either because it is man's most formidable foe, or because it is the last with which he has to contend on this side the grave, or because there is a peculiar fitness in mentioning it when the Apostle is treating of the resurrection. Perhaps all three motives may have contributed to make St. Paul's statement what it is. But there is certainly no allusion to any interval between the resurrection of the righteous and that of the wicked.

The considerations now adduced help us to answer another question which, though so far as we have observed not raised by the commentators, is one of great interest. Why does the Apostle, when He speaks in ver. 23 of the resurrection of "them that are Christ's," add the words "at His presence" ($\pi\alpha\rho\text{ου}\sigma\text{ί}\alpha$)—that is, at the glorious manifestation of His presence, commonly, though erroneously, called His "Second Coming"? Why is the raising up of the saints so long delayed? Christ rose from the dead on the third day. Why do years and centuries and tens of centuries pass before His people rise? The answer to this question connects itself with some of the most striking views presented to us in Scripture of the plan of the Almighty's dealings with His people, while it also explains to us that giving up of the kingdom by our Lord at "the end" which so greatly perplexes many a Christian reader.

For why is it that Christians do not rise until their Lord comes again? It is because the "reign" of their Head here spoken of is His reign for the overthrow of everything that opposes itself to the truth and righteousness which are in Him. It is a reign in which He puts down and brings to nought all rule and authority and power, and even death, the last enemy which man has to encounter in his present pilgrimage. Christ must reign until all these are beneath His feet. This is the reign *now* of the once crucified Redeemer. On earth He laid the foundation of His victory, and forged the weapons with which it is to be won. In heaven He uses the weapons, and rides forth to the war from which He is to return in triumph. *But He does not ride forth alone.* He does not work by His Spirit directly and immediately upon a sinful world. He does it by means of that Body which He has left behind Him *upon earth.* He summons that Body into the field, clothes it with His strength, endows it with His Spirit, takes His place, although invisible, at its head, and sends it forth to a perpetual conflict with every form of sin and misery with which earth is filled.

Let us open our eyes and look at the present position of Christ and of His people in the world. *This is not His rest; and it is not theirs.* There is a warfare to be waged, and they must wage it. There is ignorance to be enlightened, and they must enlighten it; error to be corrected, and they must correct it; sorrow to be healed, and they must heal it; all that is holy and full of blessedness for man to be introduced, and they must introduce it. The very power of death has to be destroyed, and they must destroy it, till the world is penetrated by the heavenly life which they proclaim, and death shall be no more. We speak of the infinite rest and peace which the Man of conflict and of sorrows now enjoys at the right hand of God, of the rest and peace which His people, still continuing their pilgrimage, have in Him. It is a one-sided view of their position; for the struggle with evil in the world is not yet ended, and the victory over it is not yet won.

But now, let us observe, all this warfare is to be carried on by Christ through and in that Body of His which lives on from age to age in the world. Departed saints are to have no share in the conflict. They may watch it, but they are not upon the field. Like a great cloud of witnesses they may surround us, but their own race is run, their own warfare is over, their burden of toil is thrown aside; they rest. Rest, however, they could not, were they already raised, for then they would accompany the Saviour, and the plan of the campaign would be destroyed. Therefore not now, but only at His Coming, are they raised; when, having rested after the toils of their own day, they shall join the whole army which like them has fought and conquered.

What has been said goes also far to explain the statement of the Apostle as to the delivering up of Christ's kingdom to God, even the Father. For this delivering up of the kingdom is the immediate consequence of the ending of the reign; and the reign, as we have seen, consisted in putting down all the enemies of God and man. When these enemies are put down, there is no more need for this particular "reign;" there is nothing upon which its power is to be exercised. It therefore closes, and the kingdom connected with it is delivered up. In one sense

Christ never ceases to be a King. He is a King upon His throne. He is set down with His Father upon His throne. Of His Kingdom there shall be no end. Throughout eternity the whole army of the redeemed shall follow Him, and shall read upon His vesture and upon His thigh this name written— "King of kings and Lord of lords." But then He shall be their King only to bless them with His presence, and to bestow upon them, with the large liberality that becomes Him, His royal favours. In the new heavens and the new earth wherein dwelleth righteousness He has no enemies to subdue, and in that sense no "reign," no "kingdom," to continue.

Hence, accordingly, the words of vers. 27 and 28: "But when He saith, All things are put in subjection, it is evident that He is excepted who did subject all things unto Him. And when all things have been subjected unto Him, then shall the Son also Himself be subjected to Him that did subject all things unto Him, that God may be all in all." It is obvious that He who is here spoken of as God is the same as He who is described in ver. 24 as "God, even the Father," so that the meaning is, not simply that the Almighty in His infinite power and absolute sovereignty, but as. Father, shall be all in all. In other words, when the Son shall have executed His commission of revealing the Father, and shall have carried home that revelation to the hearts of all, there will be nothing to interfere with the universal song of praise that shall ascend alike from Him and them to His Father and their Father, to His God and their 'God. It is as if a sovereign were to send forth some illustrious commander to subdue a distant and rebellious portion of his kingdom. That commander would never cease to be subject to his sovereign's will, or to receive and carry out the instructions that had been put into his hands. Yet the eyes of the loyal subjects of the kingdom would be fastened on him, even as a servant. They would watch eagerly for tidings as to his plans or his successes. Their thoughts would be with him in the council chamber and in the field. Even the gracious rule of their sovereign at home would for the time be less than usual the subject of their thoughts or the theme of their acclamations. At length, however, the rebellion is put down, the disloyal forces are scattered, peace and order are restored, and the commander, who has accomplished all, returns to give an account of his stewardship, and to lay down his sheathed sword at his sovereign's feet. Then the peaceful and orderly administration of the empire goes forward undisturbed; and as law is administered with justice, as order is maintained with firmness, as the arts of peace prosper and every feeling of insecurity is dispelled, the minds of men return without distraction to their sovereign, and they acknowledge him to be the one centre around which gather all the interests of their political and national life. Something of this kind is the course of the Apostle's thought in the words before us. The Son returns victorious from the field, and God, even the Father, is all in all. Everywhere there is a Father's love, everywhere the outpouring of the blessings of a Father's hand, there is nothing to hurt nor to destroy in all the holy mountain of the Lord.

Thus, then, has St. Paul unfolded the whole plan of God's dealings with His people, until eternity itself is reached. Nor need it be objected that the description is incomplete, inasmuch as there is no mention of the lost, of the devil and his angels and wicked men. It is characteristic of the Apostle to say nothing of them. He leaves them in the hands of God—to stand or fall to their own Master. What have I to do, he would exclaim, to judge them that are without? I deal only with them that are within; and it is enough for me to look forward to a time when the Lord shall reign among His people gloriously, when creation itself shall be delivered from the bondage of corruption, and when the Father and the Father's love shall, so far as my eye reaches, be all in all.

"Else what shall they do which are baptized for the dead? If the dead are not raised at all, why then are they baptized for them? why do we also stand in jeopardy every hour? I protest by that glorying in you, brethren, which I have in Christ Jesus our Lord, I die daily. If after the manner of men I fought with beasts at Ephesus, what doth it profit me?—1 COR. XV. 29-32A. [R.V.]

Chapter v.

IT is often imagined either that the paragraph of this chapter preceding that upon which we now enter, and extending from ver. 20 to ver. 28, is a digression on the part of St. Paul from the main line of his argument; or that, at the point reached by us, some fresh thought suddenly occurs to the Apostle which connects itself, not with what he had just said, but with his former description—vers. 12-19—of the miserable consequences of denying the great truth with which he was engaged. Thus regarded, the verses beginning with the 29th are separated from those immediately preceding them; and the interpretation of a passage, difficult enough in itself and under any circumstances, is rendered still more difficult. But the word "Else," of ver. 29, is conclusive against any such view of the connexion. That word shows that there is no break in the thought of the Apostle at the point where it occurs, and that there is no return to a line of reflection with which he had been engaged some verses before. All that it introduces in vers. 29-34 is directly and immediately related to what had just been said of the nature of Christ's reign, and of the time and manner of its termination. The word, opening as it does the next following sentence, would lose its meaning were it not so. That particle is one of those important links of thought to which the interpreter is bound to render justice.

The importance of this remark will appear by and by. In the meanwhile, simply keeping it in mind, we may proceed to consider the obscure words of ver. 29 —" Else what shall they do which are baptized for the dead? If the dead are not raised at all, why then are they baptized for them?"

Few words of the New Testament have occasioned greater perplexity than these, and few have received more numerous or more discordant interpretations. To discuss all the latter is impossible, nor would any good end be served by the attempt. They are in general too artificial and far-fetched, as when it is suggested that the words refer to baptism over the graves of the dead (Luther), or to the washing of the dead body (Beza), or to the removal of ceremonial defilement contracted by touching the dead (Ewald). Or they suppose an amount of ellipsis and abbreviation which it is impossible to accept, as when the clause " for the dead " is understood to mean a confession of faith in the resurrection of the dead supposed to have been made at baptism, and by which therefore those who had not renounced their baptism, though they were denying the resurrection, were self-convicted (Hammond). Or they put a meaning into the word "dead" out of keeping with the whole tone of St. Paul's argument in this chapter, understanding by it not the actually dead, but the dead in sin (Hofmann). Upon interpretations such as these it is unnecessary to dwell.

It would seem also that we may be justified in saying little of the ancient patristic interpretation recently revived and defended with his usual vigour and spirit by Canon Evans in the *Speaker's Commentary*. According to it, the words before us mean " with a view to the resurrection of the dead," the preposition ὑπέρ being absolutely neutral in sense, conveying no thought of benefit or advantage to the dead, and expressing only the fact that the ulterior view of a neophyte's mind as he bent over the long roll or class of the dead was their resurrection. With respect to, with an eye upon, a similar resurrection he was then himself baptized, and to deny the resurrection was thus a denial of his baptism. But this neutral sense of ὑπέρ is altogether unproved. It may border upon περί, just as it borders also upon ἀντί, but it will, we believe, be invariably found that the true force of the preposition, " for the advantage of," " for the good of," enters more or less into its meaning. Besides which, the principle of abbreviation used in common speech does not apply in cases where the abbreviated sentence has a *definite meaning of its own*, distinct from that of the sentence which for our own convenience we have shortened. We may certainly abbreviate where there is no danger of mistake, as was the case with the sentence of his lady friend in which Canon Evans finds an instance of breviloquence somewhat similar to that which he here discovers in the Apostle. No one could misunderstand her. But when an abbreviated sentence, taken by itself, has a clear and definite sense, though it may be one not at first fully comprehended by us, a speaker or writer is not entitled to substitute it for the full utterance of his thought, lest in doing so he lead us astray. Now nothing can be clearer than that this is the case here. "Such an one has been baptized for the dead" is a sentence complete as it stands. We may not fully comprehend it, but to substitute for it another sentence, "Such an one has been baptized with a view to the resurrection of the dead," is to claim a freedom of interpretation which the laws of language refuse to grant. The refusal, too, is enforced in the present instance by the immediate repetition of the thought —"Why are they then baptized for them?" This interpretation must follow in the wake of those that have preceded it.

There are, however, two interpretations of an entirely different kind, which deserve longer notice, for the sake either of their own intrinsic beauty, or of the great names by which they are supported.

1. The first of these is due to Olshausen. That critic starts with the supposition that ὑπέρ cannot here mean "instead of," but must be understood in the sense of "to the advantage of;" and then, connecting the words before us closely with ver. 23, where we are told that Christ is the first-fruits of them that

sleep, and that after Him they shall rise who shall be His at His Coming, he supposes that the Apostle refers to the filling up of an appointed number of the members of Christ's Body, which must be completed before the end. "Inasmuch as a certain number, a πλήρωμα, of believers is required, which must be complete before the *Parousia* (and with it the resurrection) can take place, every one who receives baptism benefits thereby the body of believers, those already dead in the Lord" (*in loc.*). Olshausen, however, is afterwards constrained to allow that this idea bears so remotely on the subject that St. Paul could not justly assume that it would be correctly understood by all his readers, and he suggests the following modification of it. He would now receive ὑπέρ as equivalent to ἀντί in the signification "instead of," "in place of," which he says "presents no difficulty:" and then, applying as before the words "the dead" to departed believers, he obtains the meaning that those who "are baptized for the dead" are new members of the Christian community coming in to supply the place of its deceased members, and who, it might well be said, would gain nothing thereby were there no resurrection of the dead. By this suggestion of Olshausen's we are to conceive of Christians, as of an army in the field of battle where, as the front rank falls, the second rank steps in and takes its place. Why should they do this? the Apostle asks; Why should new soldiers of the cross thus fill up the ranks that have been thinned by the foe, if the fallen do not rise again? It must be allowed that the interpretation is one of interest and beauty; and later inquirers have sought to strengthen it by quoting at least one instance from a classical author, in which the preposition ὑπέρ appears to be used with reference to the enlisting of soldiers in the room of such as had perished in war, and thus in the very sense thought so suitable here. Notwithstanding this, we must urge that the two prepositions of which we have been speaking are never simply interchangeable with one another, and that with ὑπέρ, which meets us in the present passage, the idea of conferring benefit on the persons alluded to is always associated. In this respect Olshausen's second suggestion, and that in which he finally took refuge, fails. His first, though doubted by himself, is by much the more important of the two, and we shall immediately avail ourselves of the help afforded by it in endeavouring to discover the Apostle's meaning.

2. The second interpretation of which we have to speak supposes that in the words before us we have an allusion to vicarious baptism. There is reason to believe that towards the end of the second century such baptism existed. Passing over what we have been told by Chrysostom of the foolish custom of the followers of Marcion, it would seem that some of the heretical sects of the second century recognised the propriety of vicarious baptism in the case of catechumens who had died before they could be brought to the baptismal font. A person came forward in

the place of the departed catechumen, and, making confession of sin and receiving the water of baptism in his stead, transferred the benefit of the sacramental rite from himself to the individual whom he represented. The argument of St. Paul upon this supposition is that, if the dead do not rise to eternal life, such vicarious baptism would be meaningless. The fact of its administration was therefore a proof to those among whom the practice existed that, whether they thought of it or not, they did allow that the dead would be raised up.

The contention therefore is that, startling as at first sight such an argument may be, it is not impossible that St. Paul might have had recourse to it. It might have been a kind of *argumentum ad hominem*, an argument not wholly valid in itself, but the force of which would be felt by his opponents, because they could not deny that the practice in question must rest upon a principle, and because there could be no doubt as to what the principle in this case involved. Such arguments are often legitimately employed in common life, and what is consistent with true reasoning there is not less consistent with true reasoning in religious life. Further, it is pleaded that, gross as was the superstition involved in this vicarious baptism, there was yet something in it so very natural that it might perhaps have disarmed the indignation with which we should have expected the Apostle to regard it. And, finally, it is urged that after all St. Paul shows by his language that he does separate himself from those who practised such a rite. Throughout the whole of the rest of the passage he uses the pronouns "we" and "I" and "you." "Why do *we* also stand in jeopardy every hour?" "If *I* fought with beasts at Ephesus;" "*I* die daily;" "I protest by that glorying in *you* which I have in Christ Jesus." But here there is a change, "What shall *they* do which are baptized for the dead?" "Why then are *they* baptized for them?" And the change would almost seem to indicate that with these persons the Apostle refuses to connect himself. He says not what shall *we* do? what shall *you* do? but what shall *they* do? *They* have a certain practice. *We* have nothing to do with it; but it is at all events sufficient to condemn themselves.

Notwithstanding what may thus be said, and in spite of the fact that this interpretation has found more favour than any other in recent times, it seems impossible to adopt it.

(1.) There is not the slightest evidence that the practice of vicarious baptism existed in the days of St. Paul. The first traces of it are discovered nearly 150 years later than his time, and even then they are found only among the adherents of a small heretical sect which was marked by other grievous errors, and which never rose to any position of authority. It is true that the great orthodox Fathers of the Church describe the practice; but they do so only that they may ridicule and condemn it, while at the same time they indicate their own opinion that it was this passage misinterpreted which gave rise to the practice, not the practice which gave rise to the passage.

(2.) The words before us, so interpreted, have no real bearing upon the Apostle's reasoning. He is arguing with members of the Church, not with a heretical sect which, by adopting the practice supposed to be spoken of, would rather make both it and arguments founded upon it distasteful to true believers. Even although they who practised vicarious baptism might have their doubts as to the resurrection silenced, no effect would be produced on those who did not acknowledge the propriety of the rite referred to, or, in other words, upon the great bulk of the Christian community. Had the deniers of the resurrection at Corinth been *the same as those* who are thought to have practised vicarious baptism, the circumstances of the case would have been different, and against them the argument might have been good. But these latter persons, instead of denying, must have acknowledged the resurrection, or something like it, something, at all events, which inferred that the dead were not beyond the reach of benefit. Only on this supposition can we explain the ceremonial ascribed to them. An appeal to them, therefore, could have no effect in silencing those "among" (ver. 12) the Corinthian Christians who were in difficulty, and St. Paul was far too good a reasoner to use arguments which in their own nature could not fail to fall harmless upon his adversaries.

(3.) Whatever may be or has been said in favour of the possibility that St. Paul might allude to such a custom without condemning it, it still remains so grotesque, so superstitious, and so absurd, as to entitle us to expect that the Apostle, when he had occasion to speak of it, would not fail to indicate the light in which he must certainly have regarded it. His mere use of the word " they " by no means sufficiently separates him from those who tolerated the idea of having dead men baptized by proxy. By referring to them as he does, he rather so far marks with his approbation the course which they pursued, and it is unnecessary to say that that course was both irreconcilable with his whole system of teaching and subversive of some of the most fundamental principles of Christianity.

Nor does it at all help the matter to introduce, as Beet does, the supposition that either already baptized members of the Church or catechumens may have received the rite " in some cases at the request of the dying man, as a testimony to the Church of his faith," and simply to " supply an omission " on his part. Few things are more inconceivable than that a dying man, desirous to rectify a mistake, and to give assurance of his faith, should, instead of requesting baptism for himself, ask that another might be baptized in his place after he was dead. The whole conception of vicarious baptism must be unhesitatingly set aside. We have to try some other solution of the difficulty, and for that purpose we submit the following considerations :—

1. "The dead" spoken of in ver. 29 are unquestionably the *already baptized*, the Christian dead. This is apparent from the fact that throughout the whole chapter St. Paul does not once allude to a resurrection of unbelievers. He deals, as we have already seen distinctly at ver. 22, with believers only. The being "raised" to which he refers is always a being raised in glory. The Apostle associates no other thought with those whom he speaks of as "the dead," than that they are *followers of Christ now resting in their graves in the hope of the resurrection.*

2. Vers. 30 and 31 are not to be separated from ver. 29, as if they were the introduction of a new line of argument, as if there were a transition from the thought of one of the sacraments of the Church, which rightly viewed suggested a particular conclusion, to the thought of the ordinary struggles and trials of the Christian life, and to the bearing of the latter on those only *by* whom they were endured. In the verses of which we speak, St. Paul is still thinking of something *done for others*, as is proved, not only by the whole strain of the argument, but by his use of the word "also" in ver. 30. His thoughts are still running in the same line, and he might have spoken of his own hourly jeopardy, of his own daily deaths, as being, not less than the baptisms of ver. 29, "for the dead." Edwards, therefore, in his Commentary appears to misapprehend the sense when he gives as the meaning of ver. 30, "Not only those that get themselves baptized for the dead, but we also, who do

not, are equally with them inconsistent, if there is no resurrection of the dead." The insertion of the "we also, *who do not*," has not only no foundation in the text, but completely perverts the meaning of the καί.

3. The baptism mentioned in ver. 29 is to be taken in its most pregnant sense. There is more under it than the thought of the mere initiatory sacrament of the Christian life. It includes the thought of all to which the Christian pledged himself, the thought of the trials and sufferings which were then inseparable from the Christian profession, the thought of the self-denial and the self-sacrifice for the good of others to which, in accepting that sacrament, the Christian became bound. Not that these things are all expressly included in the word "baptize"; but as they were the necessary results of baptism, the mention of baptism brings them up before the mind.

4. The connexion of the verses under consideration with those immediately preceding is to be maintained with the utmost possible closeness. St. Paul had been speaking of the "reign" of Christ, that is, as we have already seen, not of His reign in glorious triumph, but of His reign for the destruction of His enemies, for the abolishing of "all rule and all authority and power," and even "the last enemy," death. He had been speaking, moreover, of that "reign" as of one in which Christ's saints still on earth, but not His departed saints, had a share. The departed *rest*, waiting till the whole harvest is gathered in. Their toils are over; their struggle is ended; they wait for

the finishing of the reign, for the completing of the victory. Only living saints are summoned to contend with the powers of evil, to toil, to be in jeopardy, and to die in the cause of truth and goodness. To these and such thoughts the first word of ver. 29, the word " Else," directly leads us.

Keeping then these things in mind, it seems possible to see the precise point which St. Paul has in view when he asks the questions of verse 29. The Christian dead are not yet perfected. They have not yet attained to the full rest and refreshing which has been prepared for them ; nor can they attain to it until the " reign " of Christ, carried on by means of His struggling and warring Church on earth, is finished. Every one, therefore, who enters by baptism into that Church, who takes upon him the name of Christ, and who pledges himself to a share in the contest of Christianity with the world, does so not to his own benefit only, but to the benefit of the Christian dead. He helps to bring that contest to its termination, which must be finished before the members of the Body of Christ can be clothed with perfect glory. In a strict sense of the words he is baptized, he is in jeopardy, every hour, he dies daily, for their behoof not less than for his own. But he could not do so were there no resurrection for believers, because the thought of such resurrection at the end of the contest, and introducing the joy of the new heavens and the new earth wherein dwells only righteousness, is a fundamental ingredient in his state of mind. The expectation is essentially and absolutely necessary to the sacrifice. The latter rests upon and is sustained by the former. Upon the former as upon a chief foundation the building stands; and, while it stands, we know that the foundation is secure.

Such then appears to be the thought of St. Paul in these difficult words; and it is substantially the same thought as that which he expresses when, writing to the Colossians, he says, "Now I rejoice in my sufferings for your sake, and fill up on my part that which is lacking of the afflictions of Christ in my flesh, for His body's sake which is the Church" (Col. i. 24). In both cases Christians really benefit the Church, and the same preposition, ὑπέρ, is used in both. But in the Colossian Epistle, St. Paul has his thoughts fixed upon the Church as a whole; in that to the Corinthians he is naturally led to think mainly of that portion of the Church on the prospects of which the sceptical spirit then prevalent was casting doubt. The point to be particularly noticed is that, in speaking of baptism, the Apostle does not here think of it as simply a sacrament of the Christian Church, and a seal of the Covenant of grace. He rather thinks of it as the entrance upon a struggle, a warfare, a battle with evil in all its forms, or as an enlistment in that army which our exalted Head in heaven is ever sending forth against the strongholds of sin, that by means of it He may complete His "reign;" and, so thinking of it, he asks, if all this be involved in baptism, why should fresh levies be constantly baptized? We can understand it if they are hastening on the glory of the end, and so coming to the help of "the dead," who cannot apart from them be made perfect. But on any other supposition their warfare would be without an aim, and could have no other issue than disappointment and defeat.

The very same thought continues to occupy the mind of the Apostle in the 30th and 31st verses: "Why do we also stand in jeopardy every hour? I protest by your glorying, brethren, which I have in Christ Jesus our Lord, I die daily. If after the manner of men I fought with beasts at Ephesus, what shall it profit me?" Two considerations may be worth noting as tending to prove that in these words we have no introduction of an entirely new line of thought, but that St. Paul is still dwelling upon privileges and blessings to be realized not now, but at the Second Coming of the Lord. First, there is in ver. 30 the copulative "also" of which we have already spoken; and secondly, there is the mention of that "glorying" in the progress of the gospel among the Corinthians which St. Paul "*has* in Christ Jesus our Lord." The thought is almost exactly the same as that of 1 Thess. ii. 19, 20, "For what is our hope, or joy, or crown of glorying? Are not even ye before our Lord Jesus at His coming? For ye are our glory and our joy." In other words, then, the Apostle "has," possesses even now, laid up in Christ, and waiting for manifestation, that glorying in the Corinthian Christians which would eventually be his great reward in return for the deaths

on their behalf which he was dying daily. His line
of thought is precisely similar to that in ver. 29.
The battle is still before his eyes; he only turns from
the general army to himself and his fellow-labourers
in the ministry of Christ. They were every hour in
danger. At Ephesus more particularly, where he had
lived for nearly three years, he had himself experienced
constant toil, and had been beset by the most un-
scrupulous and bloodthirsty foes. The tumult raised
by Demetrius and his craftsmen had been but a
sample of his trials there. Again and again had his
enemies attacked him as if they had been wild beasts,
the city the arena of an amphitheatre, and he the
doomed victim of antichristian rage. His had been
no peaceful ministry, no leading of his little flock to
green pastures and still waters. He had been compelled to feel that God had set forth the Apostles last
of all as men doomed to death, for they were made " a
spectacle to the world, both to angels and to men " (1
Cor. iv. 9). Yet it is the thought of these afflictions
as endured *for the good of others*, and not in their
bearing only upon himself and his fellow-labourers,
that is still in the Apostle's mind. It is the " glorying " of the Church of Christ, or of that portion of it
which he has served, that shines before him as his
reward. It is *their* resurrection, not *his own*, though
he too must rise to share it, that appears to him as
his reward. *Their* loss of the eternal crown rather
than *his* loss of it will deprive him of his " profit."
In other words, the thought of " the dead," of the

Christian dead, is still before him. He is fighting the Church's battle. He is winning the Church's victory. But all this implied the resurrection of the dead. Why should he and others endure all these struggles were there no resurrection and no hereafter? If their hope of sharing the glory prepared for the Risen Lord after His struggle was a delusion, their life and labours were a mistake, and the Apostle immediately proceeds to unfold this thought.

" If the dead are not raised, let us eat and drink, for to-morrow we die. Be not deceived : Evil company doth corrupt good manners. Awake up righteously, and sin not ; for some have no knowledge of God : I speak this *to move you to shame.*"—1 Cor. xv. 32B-34. [R.V.]

Chapter vi.

IT was a noble life lived for a noble aim which the Apostle had connected with the hope of the resurrection—a life of toil, of struggle, of self-denial, and self-sacrifice, in order to put down evil and to make good triumphant, in order to hasten on a time when Christ's victory should be fully gained, and when, all opposing forces having been subjected to the Son, the Son also should be subjected to Him that did subject all things unto Him, that God might be all in all. But what if there were no resurrection, if Christ were not raised, and if His people had no well-grounded hope of being in due season raised up with Him ? Where would their life be then ? Its aims, its motives, its encouragements lost, what effect would inevitably follow ? The answer is given in the last half of ver. 32 : " If the dead are not raised, let us eat and drink, for to-morrow we die."

The words startle us much in the same way as did the words of ver. 19, " If in this life only we have hoped in Christ, we are of all men most pitiable." Does St. Paul really mean that, if there be no resurrection of the dead, we may as well abandon ourselves to the unrestrained enjoyment of all that this world can afford? Does he mean that, in that case, it will be the course of wisdom to give scope to every appetite, and the rein to every passion; and that, if we have no hope of the future, we may be justified in yielding to every animal inclination, until we sink to the level, and even far lower than the level, of the beasts that perish? It is not in the least degree necessary to think so. His words are a quotation from the Old Testament, from Isa. xxii. 13. They are the despairing cry of the inhabitants of Jerusalem at a time when they were besieged by the Assyrians, and when the city was on the verge of ruin. "In that day," according to the representation of the prophet in ver. 12, "did the Lord, the Lord of Hosts, call to weeping, and to mourning, and to baldness, and to girding with sackcloth." But, instead of listening to the divine voice, the city rushed to the opposite extreme: "Behold joy and gladness, slaying oxen and killing sheep, eating flesh and drinking wine: let us eat and drink, for tomorrow we shall die" (ver. 13). The words were those of men who were steeling themselves against the divine warnings; who were untouched by the seriousness of their position, or the thought of their impending fate; and who, at a moment when their circumstances demanded a more than ordinary degree of serious reflection, were abandoning themselves to lightness and folly, to the song and to the dance. There is no need therefore to think that the words include the love of coarse pleasures or vicious indulgence. We put into them all the meaning that is demanded either by their original position, or as quoted by St. Paul, if we suppose them to imply no more than this, that, without the hope of continued existence beyond the grave, life is in danger of losing all its earnestness both of thought and purpose. A life without hope of the resurrection is contrasted with a life that has such hope; and we are told that the one leads us simply to enjoy ourselves, that by the other alone are we reminded that we have a higher nature and nobler duties.

We may well ask, Is the contrast true? Is it really the case that, without the hope of another and a higher world, our life here would soon sink into a mere life of sensuous enjoyment, of making the most of the pleasures that fleet past us with such rapidity, and of avoiding the struggle, the pain, and the disappointments that must be experienced by the man who lives for others than himself? The fact cannot be denied, that at this moment there is hardly any religious truth in regard to which a greater amount of uncertainty prevails than in regard to the doctrine of a personal immortality, and the importance of that doctrine to a high estimate of man's present life. There are many whom the thought of annihilation at death does not affect with the shrinking or the horror with which at one time it filled the mind. There are many who, perplexed by the vicissitudes of fortune, and wearied with the struggle of the world, simply long for rest in the grave. And there are certainly not a few who urge, that belief in a corporate immortality has a far more animating and elevating power than belief in an immortality that is personal. " In the thought of an endless progress of the race," they say, " there is something far nobler, far less selfish, and it may be found of stronger stimulus to exertion, than either the hope of individual immortality or the thirst for posthumous fame."[1] To fix our hope upon another world rather tends, they would add, to draw us away from the duties of the world in which we live. Nay, without the hope of immortality we may feel more keenly for the poor and wretched than we shall be able to do when we dwell upon a future which is to see all wrong redressed and all virtuous sorrow healed.

Is it really so ? The question is so important that it may be well to devote to it a little more attention than the ordinary course of exposition would demand. In doing so, we are not called upon to deny that there may often be much truth in statements such as those that have been referred to. It is undoubtedly the fact that individual instances may be produced in which the contemplation of the world beyond the grave has been so intense as to absorb every longing and effort of the soul ; although even then it would still hold good that, if the thought of a blessed existence in

[1] Professor Hodgson in his *Life and Letters* by Meiklejohn.

the future elevates at all, that thought carried to excess may at least stir up to imitate it persons whom nothing but excess can move. In like manner, it may be urged that the expectation of future judgment on the oppressor may be so cherished as to make us less anxious than we might otherwise be that judgment shall overtake him now. Or it may even be pleaded that one who is insensible to the grandeur of humanity at large can have no just impression of those divine considerations relating to the individual by which he professes to be guided. Yet, apart from all this, we have every reason to acknowledge the force of the strong language of the Apostle when he gives it as his alternative to the hope of individual and personal immortality: " Let us eat and drink, for to-morrow we shall die." For—

1. It is well to notice the precise nature of that hope of which he speaks. Were the immortality anticipated in this chapter simply sensuous enjoyment continued through everlasting ages ; were the rest to which it refers a mere rest from toil, or mere deliverance from hunger and thirst and cold and pain; were that Jerusalem above, which is the goal of all our hopes, no more than a city with streets of gold and gates of pearl, where the sun never goes down, and there is no night,—it might indeed be impossible to say that the withdrawal of our hope must be attended with the fatal effect that is here ascribed to it. But such ideas have no place whatever in the Apostle's mind. Even

the resurrection of the body is not to him an isolated fact, which may be viewed apart either from its cause upon the one hand or its consequences upon the other. It is a resurrection in Christ, with Christ, and to Christ—the Lord of glory. It is the necessary condition of eternal life, and St. Paul's thoughts are mainly occupied, not with the condition, but with the life which presupposes it. That life is led in a risen Saviour. Through Him it is with God and in God, a holy, blessed, active life in communion and fellowship with Him who is the foundation of all existence and the dispenser of all happiness; and who, in the perfect sum of His glorious attributes and energies, is "all in all" (ver. 28). Nor is this life confined to the time when believers shall be raised from the grave. Their resurrection-life is the continuation and perfecting of the life now begun. Already they belong to the new line of Christ's descendants. Already they are, in a certain sense, risen with Him, and seated with Him in the heavenly places. In the world they are above the world, and the powers of the world to come are the ruling influences which they obey.

2. The effect of such a hope, therefore, is to increase, not to diminish, the value of our present life. Men may urge that the hope of a corporate as distinguished from an individual immortality has its own quickening effect. They may direct our attention to the stones which, lying around us, are insignificant when considered individually, but which

gain immeasurably in importance when their individuality is lost in some splendid building they have been used to rear. Or they may speak of the several members of the body which only reach completeness because they are not individual existences, but parts of a great whole, through which a richer, fuller life than belongs to any single member pulsates, a life which each, in its own place, helps to enlarge and to adorn. Christianity does not deny these facts. If there is one truth more distinctly brought out by it than another, it is its rejection of mere individualism, and the prominence which it assigns to the arrangement that we are every one members one of another. By nothing more than her failure to recognise this with the emphasis that is due to it is the Church of Christ at this moment weakened. But surely before we can speak of " every one " joined to every other in a complete and beautiful totality, we must have established the separate existence and value of the " one." It has been always and justly regarded as not the least inestimable service which the Christian faith has rendered to humanity, that it brought out, as it did, the worth of the individual. To man as man it first addressed itself; and in that circumstance alone lay the germ of the greatest and most beneficial revolution which the world has seen. Men had felt before the value of empires, of single peoples, of armies, of crowds, of vassals. They had never felt the value of man, apart from the mass of which each was but one small item, or separated from all those adventitious circumstances that might distinguish him amidst his fellows. Christianity taught the worth of the human soul. "For what shall a man be profited," it said, "if he shall gain the whole world and forfeit his soul? Or what shall a man give in exchange for his soul?" That single soul is more valuable than all outward things, and it is so, because it is a soul; not because it is rich or mighty or learned, but because it is a soul; because in the lowest depths of poverty, utterly unknown to fame, bound even with the fetters of the slave, it has within it a spark of the Divine, can hold communion with the Infinite, and is destined for immortality. By this single lesson the Redeemer of the world burst the icy crust in which our fertile mother-earth was bound, and the little blades of grass and flowers of spring could everywhere look up and smile. In this a new starting-point for the regeneration of humanity was given, and he who received the lesson lifted his head, and felt what it was to be a man.

Analogies, therefore, from the stones of the field or the members of the body are falsely used when they are used to make us undervalue the importance of individual life. Individual life comes first; and, if it be no doubt true that the complete life of the whole adds a value to the life of the individual which it would not otherwise possess, it is not less true that the value of an organized whole is dependent upon the organized perfection of each of its individual parts.

But this perfection is greatly marred if the life of

the individual does not stretch into another and a better world. Is it for nothing that the vanity of this life has been the constant theme of the moralist and the poet? Or have those who, without hope of immortality, have tried most to solve the riddle of human existence, done injustice to the world when they have not only proclaimed it to be vain, but have denounced it as constituted as much for the misery as for the happiness of the race? Is the alternative wholly wrong that has been presented to us from this point of view—that either God is not all-powerful, not able to accomplish whatever He desires, or that He is not benevolent, not One who would promote above everything else the welfare and happiness of His creatures? These are the thoughts of that modern philosophy which denies individuality of existence beyond the grave; and, left to work out their legitimate results, they will certainly make the present life not so much like the future a blank, as a dark and terrible reality from which every tender spirit must become eager to escape. If what is now often urged upon us be true, we shall need to utter a sterner and more piercing cry than that of the Psalmist, " Surely every man walketh in a vain show ; surely he disquieteth himself in vain," and life will soon weigh us down like an incubus that we shall be unable to throw off. Strange irony of thought! Those who refuse the hope of individual immortality tell us that that hope deadens us to the value of the present; and, lo! their own system leads us past that point to the still more terrible conclusion, that human life is not only a dream in which we are betrayed and cheated by a thousand phantasies, but that it is a nightmare which oppresses us with an intolerable load of anguish.

By taking away the hope of the resurrection, therefore, we do not merely deprive men of the prospect of a glorious recompense hereafter, we change the whole character of their present life. We alter the very conception of what living means. Life is no longer a high gift of God to be filled with His presence. It is something wholly separated from Him, confused, perplexed, troubled, darkened, not only cut short at death when we must bid farewell to all the interests of earth but so bounded by these interests now that it shall be hardly possible for us to rise to higher thoughts than the supply of our own immediate earthly wants.

3. Not only, however, is our individual life lowered when we abandon hope of the resurrection, we are deprived also of the most powerful motives to exertion on behalf of others. For what is it that at once arouses our deepest interest in men, and awakens within us the most earnest desire to bring them to a life of holiness and conformity to the Divine will? Is it not the thought of the hereafter, and of what may there be either gained or lost? We need not deny that the consideration of what may be done for men's present life, even allowing that their present life were all, may lead

to many an earnest effort to correct their errors, to heal their sorrows, and to elevate them in the scale of humanity. But it is when we call to mind the infinite possibilities that are wrapped up in every human soul; when we think that in each son and daughter of our race there are powers and capacities which neither earth nor time can limit; when we regard our fellow-creatures as destined for everlasting happiness, if they will only cultivate their true nature, and enter into communion with Him who made them for Himself,—it is then that we rise to a just sense of their immeasurable importance, and can comprehend the fact that even among the angels of God there should be joy over one sinner that repenteth. Animated by that thought, we can go down into the lowest depths of sin and misery, and meet every difficulty or discouragement if thus only we may bring them to a higher life.

On the other hand, let us look upon them as sometimes but little raised above the beasts that perish, or as in many a case sunk far beneath them; let us regard them as mere leaves of a tree, green for a little time, and then destined to sink into corruption that they may make way for others, and how much shall we be tempted to leave them to themselves, and to the operation of the inexorable laws of nature amidst which their lot is cast! Nature has her own methods of disposing of the profligate, of clearing out old races and opening up paths for new ones. She has sickness and disease, fire and the sword, the earthquake and the whirlwind. She has death, the great scavenger, at her command. Why not be content with these instruments? Why not help rather than hinder them? Why not rejoice in the conflagration, in the ravages of war, in any agency that is destructive to human life, and that promises to sweep away the weak and miserable? Why also not condemn the opposite course as a false and foolish sentimentalism? It may seem hard to say it, but it is difficult to resist the conviction that not a few of those who would lead the thought of our day without the lessons of religion must regard the work of our Christian and benevolent societies, our plans for the preservation of native races, and our schemes for the conversion of the heathen, as little better than an interruption to the work of Nature, who is seeking in her own way to extinguish the old and to bring in the new. How can it be otherwise? for Nature seems most of all to say, and according to such persons she only says, that in the struggle of life the strongest ought to prevail, and that with the accomplishment of that end true progress is identified. If this be her constant lesson, and if she be all, how shall we escape the conclusion that we ought to be upon her side? We can expect nothing, therefore, from a religion of Nature, or, in other words, from a religion without the hope of immortality, than that she shall lay her cold hand upon every generous emotion, and upon every self-sacrificing effort for the good of others.

4. Experience confirms what has been said. We have no right to appeal, in a question of this kind, to the lofty sentiments and even the unsparing efforts for the good of others that have marked one or two of those around us who have cast aside Christian hope. These persons may not have really done so to the extent imagined by themselves. If an old Father of the Church describes some of those who lived before the Christian era as Christians before Christ, may we not say that there have been Christians after Christ who refused to know Him; who refused, that is, to know Him in the light, most probably false, in which He had been presented to them? It may not have been Christ Himself that they cast aside, but rather a distorted image of Him reflected in the lessons of their teachers; while in the loftiness of their aims, in the unselfishness of their emotions, in the purity and beauty of their lives, they have been so much akin to Him that, had He only been seen by them as He is, they would have been attracted to Him like steel to a magnet. There may have been an acting of Christ and of His Spirit upon them which they attributed to a wrong source. Even as to them, too, and still more as to the greater number who do not stand so high, we ought to remember that they have been surrounded by Christian influences, brought into contact with Christian examples, and made to breathe a Christian atmosphere, to a far greater extent than they were themselves aware of. To

judge correctly here, we must go back to that paganism to which we are so often invited to return; we must take heathenism as it was before Christ came, or as it is now in lands where His name is unknown. Shall we find there a tone higher than that of the alternative presented by St. Paul? A patriot or philosopher occasionally appears to lighten the darkness, but his rays do not penetrate the mass. The centuries that followed Plato did not lead to a Platonic, as the centuries that followed Christ led to a Christian civilisation.

There is a tendency, too, on the part of those who without the hope of immortality are labouring for others, to despair. Plato despaired, and the finest minds and hearts of modern times that have tried to solve the problems of life without Christian principles have despaired also. Nothing, it is well known, can be sadder than their later as compared with their earlier utterances. Full of hope at first, clouds gathered in their sky as they advanced; and, before evening fell, the darkness of night settled on the landscape.

It may be said that Christians also despond. But their sadness is of another kind. Those who are without Christianity despond because their old principles fail, and they are powerless to discover new ones. Not so believers full of Christian hope. They may mourn over the obstacles that stand in the way of the full application of their principles. In the principles themselves they have unbounded confidence. Practical experience certainly declares that with the hope of the future is bound up all generous effort after a lofty life, that with the want of it there is the greatest danger of sinking into mere sensuous enjoyment.

The Apostle means no more. It is not in the least degree necessary to suppose that he places licentious indulgence as the only alternative presented to the man who denies a personal immortality. Nor does he enter upon the question whether virtuous exertion might not be pursued under the influence of motives drawn from time alone. Probably he never asked himself whether he could struggle for himself or others without the thought of a Risen Saviour, of a judgment, and of a life to come. His whole life may show us that he would have done this. But if, while doing it, he had begun to analyse his own feelings, he would have said, "It is not I, it is something else, though I know not what, that dwelleth in me;" and he would have ended in returning to the thought that what was moving him must proceed from some other quarter than himself, that it must come from a higher world, and that could he be convinced that there was no such world, he would have doubted himself, his brethren, everything—and in the doubt would have found it hard to resist the maxim that was always ringing in his ears, "Let us eat and drink, for to-morrow we shall die."

We have lingered long upon these words, but one other remark may be made before we pass on, The unselfishness of a corporate, as distinguished from a personal, immortality is often proclaimed to us. In the light of the interpretation, which in our last paper we found it necessary to give to vers. 29-31, it is really, in one great sense, a corporate immortality of which St. Paul is speaking. He is not thinking of himself only, or of saving his own soul: he is not setting before those to whom he writes the duty of saving their own souls, or of securing their own portion in the heavenly inheritance. His argument is precisely the reverse. He is thinking of the souls of others, of the Christian dead who cannot be perfected until Christ's "reign" for the destruction of all hostile powers is closed, until the kingdom of the world becomes the kingdom of our Lord and of His Christ. His whole mind is occupied with the multitude of his fellow-believers, and he longs for the hour when they, now resting in their graves, shall be men again in the full enjoyment of the heavenly reward. He sees, not so much himself rescued from destruction and safe in isolated enjoyment, as the "Mount Zion, the city of the living God, the heavenly Jerusalem, the innumerable hosts of angels, the general assembly and Church of the first-born who are enrolled in heaven, God the Judge of all, the spirits of just men made perfect, Jesus the Mediator of the New Covenant, and the blood of sprinkling that speaketh better than that of Abel." That is St. Paul's corporate immortality, an immortality in which each, as he dies, is not lost in a formless mist, but one in which all together constitute one great company, knowing and being known, loving and being loved, heart answering to heart and eye to eye for ever.

With the 32nd verse of the chapter the Apostle closes all he has to say upon the *fact* of the resurrection of the dead. But, as his mind is filled with the thought of the disastrous consequences flowing from the denial of the fact, he cannot pass on to the *manner* of the resurrection, without a solemn practical warning to the Corinthian Church. This warning is contained in the 33rd and 34th verses of the chapter. It is unnecessary to dwell at any length upon them; and it may be enough to remark that the word "manners" is to be understood of the inward disposition, not the outward demeanour, and that the warning is intended to apply to the whole Church, and not to those alone by whom the resurrection was denied.

But it is not enough to avoid evil company, and hence the precept is added—" Awake up in a righteous way, and sin not." The words of the original can hardly be so translated as to convey a full idea of their meaning. "Awake" suggests only the thought of having been asleep, while St. Paul has in his mind the sleep of drunkenness; and again, the next word of the original does not mean, with the Authorized Version, "to righteousness," while the "awake up righteously" of the Revised Version is not easily understood. The true meaning seems to be, Rouse yourselves out of your dull, heavy sleep in a righteous way, in a way that will lead to righteousness, and not to your besotting yourselves again with draughts of sinful pleasure. Let this be done once for all by a decided and determined effort (compare the tense of the verb); and then, after that, do not continue to sin (compare again the tense of the verb); but let your progress be worthy of your beginning, your later steps of your first. Thus, instead of being blinded by evil company to the light of the gospel, your eyes will be purged to behold it in all its purity. In company with the righteous, you will follow after righteousness, and God will prosper you. "Thou meetest him that rejoiceth and worketh righteousness; those that remember Thee in Thy ways;" "The meek will He guide in judgment, and the meek will He teach His way;" "The pure in heart shall see God;" "If any man willeth to do His will, he shall know of the teaching whether it be of God" (Isa. lxiv. 5; Ps. xxv. 9; Matt. v. 8; John vii. 17).

There is all the more reason to do this that there are "some" who "have no knowledge of God." How full of charity are the words! *Some* have no knowledge of God. Was not Corinth rather crowded with persons of this description? Was it not a city than which hardly any city could at that time be found more idolatrous or more debased in its idolatry? And were not the members of its Christian community among the foolish, the weak, the base, the despised, the things that were not, in comparison with the wise, the strong, the noble, the honoured, the things that were (chap. i. 26-28)? Yet, says St. Paul, "Some have no knowledge of God." One would think that almost the whole city must have been Christian. It is only the charity of the Apostle that leads him to speak thus,—a charity that grows as the heart becomes more full of Christ, leading its possessor to believe all and to hope all, to trust that even where there may be nothing but darkness to us there may be light to Him who seeth not as man seeth, and that things may turn out to be less bad than they seem. This charity, this looking at things in the best light, neither made St. Paul less fervent in prayer nor less earnest in effort for man's good.

Finally, the Apostle adds, "I speak this to your shame," *i.e.* not that I may reproach or scorn you, but that you may be ashamed of yourselves, that you may see how foolish you have been, and may in future act a wiser part.

Thus, with practical exhortation, the Apostle ends the first great half of his argument. We shall find that he does the same with the second half. He may well do so. The grand idea of practical righteousness is not an idea foisted into the writings of St. Paul by those who in our day desire to honour and uphold him, but cannot stand his doctrinal teaching. The idea is there,—there with a depth and intensity which it is utterly impossible to overstate. But it is not there to the exclusion of the doctrine. It is rather there to establish, to magnify, and to crown the doctrine.

" But some one will say, How are the dead raised? and with what manner of body do they come? Thou foolish one, that which thou thyself sowest is not quickened, except it die: and that which thou sowest, thou sowest not the body that shall be, but a bare grain, it may chance of wheat, or of some other kind; but God giveth it a body even as it pleased him, and to each seed a body of its own. All flesh is not the same flesh: but there is one flesh *of men, and another flesh of beasts, and another flesh of birds, and another of fishes. There are also celestial bodies, and bodies terrestrial: but the glory of the celestial is one, and the* glory *of the terrestrial is another. There is one glory of the sun, and another glory of the moon, and another glory of the stars; for one star differeth from another star in glory."*—1 COR. xv. 35-41. [R.V.]

Chapter vii.

THE Apostle has established in the earlier portion of this chapter the resurrection of believers, by the Resurrection of Christ. That Christ was risen was admitted without hesitation by those to whom he wrote. Their whole faith rested upon the conviction, not only that the Lord in whom they believed had died, but on the further truth, that He had been raised again, "according to the Scriptures" (ver. 4). In so far therefore as St. Paul had dwelt upon the fact, and even upon the remarkable chain of evidence by which it was established, he had done this, not so much for the purpose of proving it, as for the purpose of reinvigorating his readers' faith, and of bringing the Resurrection of Jesus home to them with liveliness and power. Hence also the degree to which he had enlarged upon the disastrous consequences that would flow to Christian faith and life in general, if Christ had not been raised.

The Corinthian Christians are now supposed to be thoroughly alive to this. No further argument upon that particular point was necessary. It followed that the universal proposition maintained at Corinth, that no one who had died would rise again, was false. One made in all points like unto His brethren had died and risen from the dead, and His brethren *might* in like manner rise. It followed not less certainly that they *would* rise. The bond of union between Christ and His people was such, that whatever befell Him must also befall them. By the arrangements of that Almighty Being who giveth no account of any of His matters, but whose dealings with His creatures are always infinitely wise and good, they had been so connected with their first parent Adam that they had inherited from him a sinful and mortal nature. It was incontestable that it was so. By a similar Divine arrangement they had inherited from "the Christ" the principle of spiritual and everlasting life; and again it was incontestable that this, not less than the former, was the case. As then they had become what the one was, so they had been made partakers of what the Other was. In the coming forth of Jesus from the grave they beheld only the Resurrection of the First-born, to be followed in due time by that of the other members of His family; the dedication of the first sheaf of harvest in the unending and joyful service of the Father, to be followed by a similar dedication of the other sheaves of the harvest-field.

The argument was closed, but difficulties still remained which might weaken its force. Questions might still be asked to which inquiring spirits might fairly expect answers. The Apostle felt that he could not neglect this aspect of the case. He must meet the difficulties, he must answer the questions; and he is to do this by an appeal to the analogy of nature. Analogy cannot indeed demonstrate, and in the passage before us it is not intended to demonstrate, that the thing reasoned about is true. Analogy can only meet a difficulty, although it may do this in an impressive and powerful way. When it is shown that the laws of the spiritual world have laws closely corresponding to them in the natural world, a strong presumption in their favour is instantly created. The God of grace must be the same as the God of providence, for God is one; and, although we may not understand the processes by which He works, we are prepared to believe that whatever law is met with in the latter may be expected in the former sphere. The principle lies at the bottom of our Lord's method of instruction by parable. There is unity in the whole system of the universe, and everything that illustrates and brings out that unity is probably true. Thus it is then that St. Paul proceeds to answer the difficulties suggested to him.

At ver. 35 an objector is introduced to us: "But some one will say, How are the dead raised? and with what manner of body do they come?" Have we here two questions, or one expressed in two different forms? When we turn to the answer contained in the following verses, the probability is that we have two: the first referring to the *process* of the resurrection; the second, to its *result*: the first concerned with the difficulty of imagining that a resurrection should take place at all; the second, with the difficulty of thinking how, if it is to take place, it can do so in a manner adapted to a heavenly world and existence there. That the latter thought is involved in the second question appears not only from the general strain of the reply, but from the singular use of the word "come." St. Paul does not say "come out of their graves" or "come into the world again." He says simply "come." "With what manner of body do they come?" The Coming of Christ, with whom His saints come, is in his mind; and it was not inappropriate to transfer that thought to the mind of an objector who, notwithstanding his present difficulties, believed in the Second Coming of his Lord.

The two objections taken together are most natural; nor are they less natural now than they were then. We stand by the bedside of a Christian friend who has just uttered his last word or breathed his last sigh. Still more, we stand by the open grave and see the body deposited in its last resting-place, till it is for ever hidden from our sight by the earth that has been filled in to cover it. We think of its helplessness, and of its insensibility to the sorrow of the surrounding mourners. Nay, we remember even that already the process of corruption has begun, and that but a short time will pass before dust will have returned to dust, and no member of the cherished form, no feature of the loved face, be discernible; and, when we think of all this, it is in no spirit of scepticism or scorn, but in one of deep perplexity and anxiety, that we ask, "How are the dead raised up? and with what manner of body do they come?" Satisfy us only upon that point, we exclaim, and many of our doubts will vanish. Let us see that it may be so, let us obtain some intelligent conception of the manner in which it will take place, and we shall ask no more. The chamber of death has awakened many to a purer and a nobler life. But is it not equally true, that the sight of the dead has instilled, and even now instils, into many a mind the suspicion that a resurrection is an impossibility, and that the Christianity of which it is a central part is no more than a beautiful but sad delusion? Therefore may we well try to understand what the Apostle says upon the point.

To the first question before us the answer is given in ver. 36: "Foolish one" (certainly not "thou fool" of the A.V., hardly even "thou foolish one" of the R.V.), "that which thou thyself sowest is not quickened, except it die." Every one allows that there is such a thing in nature as a quickening. We see it in the seeds which, when sown under proper conditions, spring up in new forms of life. But something precedes this change, and what is that? The Apostle answers, Death. But what again is death? We can be at no loss for a reply; for modern science has established with a certainty upon which it is impossible to cast a doubt, that in no case is the death of a body the destruction of the particles of which it had been previously composed. Nature knows nothing of annihilation. Whatever has been continues to be. It may be changed into other shapes, it may pass into other things; but it is never wholly blotted out from that state of *being* into which it has once been introduced. Death therefore is not destruction: it is simply disorganization, the dissolution of the bond which held the old particles together in their old sphere of existence, that they may enter upon a new one. Not only so. An entirely new form of life cannot be obtained, except through the disorganization of the old. As our Lord Himself said, "Except a corn of wheat fall into the ground, and die, it abideth by itself alone; but if it die, it beareth much fruit" (John xii. 24). We take a corn of wheat into our hands. It is dry and hard, a small body which will keep for many years without the slightest apparent change; and which, so long as it is thus kept, will produce nothing, although it may waste by a process of decay so slow as to be imperceptible. On the other hand, we drop it into the soil, and thus supply it with the conditions taught us by experience to be necessary for the result we are desirous to secure. Disorganization immediately begins; and, lo! instead of remaining any longer what it was, a change sets in. The husk of the seed is broken by some internal power. A little shoot issues forth in the dark bosom of the earth. That shoot parts into two directions, in one of which it goes downward, a thin, white, pulpy fibre, while in the other it pushes upward, seeks the free air of heaven, and appears as a green stalk, sending forth leaves, lengthening the stalk, and crowning it with the ear of corn. We call this a passing through death, says the Apostle. But call it by any name you please. What you really have is disorganization, decay, corruption, such a mingling of the particles of the seed with those of the surrounding soil that you cannot separate them. Yet out of that disorganization, decay, corruption, and mingling of particles, there comes a new form of life and loveliness.

It is no doubt true that the seed was never what we call dead. There was always a principle of life in it. But who shall say that there is not a principle of life in the believer which the cold hand of death cannot chill, which the power of death can only set free and not destroy ? In the infant of an hour old are there not undeveloped powers of nature ? May there not be also in it undeveloped powers of grace which no physical analysis can discover, and no principles of physiology explain ? And why may not he who has been united to a living Lord have in him some principle of life which is only emancipated when the last look is taken and the last sigh breathed ?

One remark may be made in passing. Have we not here an answer to a difficulty felt by many minds upon this point ? It is said that, whatever may be the case in the vegetable kingdom, the animal kingdom supplies us with no instance of death producing life.

"The animal creation dies; but where, in all the mouldering ruins of that empire which life once animated, is there any sign or token of its restoration?"[1] The question is a sad one; and, when we hear it, what a world of wreckage and of ruin spreads out on every side before the eye! But the answer is, In the lower animal creation there is no principle of union with the living Lord, there is no principle of life which death cannot touch. In the case of the believer it is otherwise. Christ is risen, and is at the right hand of the Father. That is the proposition from which we start. But, if He is risen and at the right hand of the Father, then just as in the seed there is a principle of life at the moment when we commit it to the soil, so in the believer, at the moment of death, there is that principle of union with an exalted Lord which is ready to spring up into quickened life when the poor frame in which it has been sheltered for a time returns to corruption.

Nor does it make any essential difference that in the one case the plant begins immediately to spring up, that in the other, centuries after centuries may pass before the quickened frame is bestowed. The seed does not immediately sprout unless it is sown; in other words, unless the conditions of God's plan are complied with. In the case of the believer the Apostle has taught us in this very chapter that one of these conditions is "at His Coming." "Each in his own order: Christ the first-fruits; then

[1] Hanna, *The Resurrection of the Dead*, p. 114.

they that are Christ's, at His Coming" (ver. 23). The time fixed in the Almighty's counsels for the rising of His saints has not yet arrived. They are not to take part in the contest which their Lord carries on by means of the saints still living in the flesh. They rest, they wait; and He can keep them safe till those conditions are supplied in the midst of which their principle of life shall be clothed with its appropriate frame.

The first question of ver. 35 has been answered; and at ver. 37 St. Paul proceeds to answer the second, "With what manner of body do they come?" It would appear from his reply that there are especially three difficulties in connexion with the matter which he feels it necessary to meet.

1. Is the body to be bestowed at the resurrection to be the same body that we possess now? It neither need nor will be so, is the Apostle's answer. It need not be so; for, if we look around us upon the works of God, we behold everywhere tokens of the inexhaustible resources of His Almighty hand. There is no limitation to His power, no end to the variety in which all things, whether in heaven or earth, are made. Look for a moment at the vegetable world. How diversified are the trees, the shrubs, the flowers, the vegetables, the grasses, the mosses of the field! There might have been a few forms only, yet there are forms without number and without end. Trace the ascending scale from the lowest to the highest; pause at any round of the ladder, and diverge into the side groups which

bear the marks of belonging to the common type—
everywhere something new, something different from
what we have seen. Let us take even two specimens
of the same species into our hand, and we shall find
that they are not the same. Submit the smallest
corresponding parts of these specimens to a close
examination, and we shall find that a similar law
holds. No two leaves of the same tree, no two blades
of grass, are in every respect the same.

In the animal world the same thing is again perceptible. The various animals of the earth, of the
air, and of the sea are all different from one another;
and how infinite is the variety of their forms! From
the huge elephant to the tiniest insect that lights upon
a leaf, from the great eagle that soars far beyond the
ken of human eye to the smallest bird that chirps upon
the spray, from leviathan, the mightiest monster that
plays in the great deep, down to the little minnow of
the brook, every conceivable variety of figure and habit
and life!

Nay, further. From the creatures of earth let us
pass to the orbs of heaven, to sun and moon and
stars; and, once more, they differ. Even to the imperfect vision of man they are distinguished from one
another. The constituent elements of each group, the
basis of the substance of each, may be the same; yet
upon that one basis is built up the infinite variety
that meets the eye upon every side. Each group
differs from other groups, and within each group the
individual objects also differ. The Apostle indeed

applies this thought only to the second group when he says that all are " flesh," yet " not the same flesh." Perhaps he did not know that the same remark might have been made as to the first; and certainly he did not know, what is one of the latest discoveries of the spectroscope, that it might have been made as to the third. But we know that, in the fundamental molecules of their nature, each group is the same. Few and simple are the materials with which the Creator works; and yet with them, above, below, around us, we see forms so utterly inexhaustible in number that the mind is bewildered in the attempt to grasp them.

What then is the conclusion ? There is no need that the body to be given us at the great day should be the same as it is now. He who has made all things has an infinite store of forms at His command.

If however our resurrection bodies *need not be* the same, neither *will they be* the same as our present bodies. Had this not been the case St. Paul would at once have said so. His argument proceeds upon the supposition that they will be different, and is only intelligible if we accept that supposition as correct. Besides this, it is plainly implied in the contrast drawn by him between the " bare grain " and the future plant. He does not bring the former into comparison with the grains of the same kind with which the ear of corn is filled, but with the whole plant which springs from it ; and to the most careless glance these are entirely unlike each other. Another comparison leading to the same conclusion is made by him in 2 Corinthians v. 1-3, when he contrasts "the earthly house of our tabernacle, to be dissolved," with the "building from God, the house not made with hands, eternal, in the heavens;" when he speaks of our "habitation which is from heaven," and anticipates the hour at which, being clothed, we shall not be found γυμνοί, the γυμνόν of the present passage. The resurrection body will not then be the body we possess now. What degree of resemblance it may have to this last, how far it may be identified with it, in what respects it may in both stages still be *ours*, may receive further elucidation as St. Paul proceeds. In the meantime we have only to do with the fact that it will not be the same. Again therefore we may stand by the bed of death or the open grave, and St. Paul will say to us, Do not perplex yourselves with the idea that the particles of that frame already returning to corruption will on the morning of the resurrection be reunited as you see them. What you see is only the outward husk of the principle of life contained in the seed. When the seed germinates it will spring up something wholly different to the outward eye.

2. The second difficulty which the Apostle has to meet is this, Will the bodies to be bestowed at the resurrection be adapted to the new condition of things then introduced? When men heard of a body to be inhabited by the spirit in the heavenly world, they naturally thought of the body possessed by them in this world. They had neither heard of nor seen any other, and no thought of any other could occur to

them. But, if so, was not this at variance with all that they otherwise knew of that better land, which was the goal of their hopes and expectations? Whatever else that land might be, it was surely a land of light and glory, of freedom from pain and sorrow and death. What harmony could there be between such a land and the present bodies of believers, wearied with toil, subject to disease, tormented with pains, liable at any moment to become the spoil of the last enemy of man? Yet what else was there to look for? Or, if we are after all persuaded that there will be a new body, what assurance have we that it will be suitable to the light and glory that we anticipate in the heavenly world? We see the answer to this difficulty in the fact that there runs through St. Paul's argument more than the thought of many forms already dwelt on. Not only is there an infinite variety of forms, but these are everywhere adapted to the scene in which they play their part. The plants and beasts of the earth, the birds of the air, and the fishes of the sea, are not only different from each other, they are also, whatever the seed or germ from which they spring, in perfect harmony with their surroundings.

It is interesting to notice the manner in which this thought comes out, incidentally rather than directly, the unpremeditated expression of a state of habitual conviction, rather than of argument, deliberately sought for and used at the moment. The word "glory" is the key to it. Why say, "There is one *glory* of the sun, and another *glory* of the moon, an another *glory* of the stars; for one star differeth from another star in *glory*." Why not rather say, There is one nature of the sun, and another nature of the moon, and another nature of the stars; for one star differeth from another? Because it is the firmament of heaven in its splendour by day, it is the star-bespangled sky by night, of which St. Paul is thinking. That firmament, that sky, is a glorious spectacle, and each orb of light that shines in it is fitted to hang from such a glowing roof; each is a glory. True, St. Paul extends the thought to things of earth, to terrestrial as well as celestial bodies, but he may do so with propriety; for "the glory of the celestial is one, and the glory of the terrestrial is another." Everywhere glory; yet not alone in the idea of the object itself, but in the idea of its adaptation to its surroundings, does the "glory" lie; and, once the mind takes hold of this idea, it sees glory everywhere. The correspondences of nature, in short, are so universal and so marked, as to assure us, that whatever body the Almighty gives His children at the Coming of the Lord will be perfectly conformable to "the new heavens and the new earth, wherein dwelleth righteousness."

The second difficulty, like the first, has been met by a consideration of the analogies supplied by nature. These analogies show us that there is no need to fear that there cannot be a resurrection body adapted to a resurrection life. He who gives to each beast and bird and fish and orb of heaven its suitableness to the sphere in which it is to move will not fail to provide that the frame destined to be the eternal home of the redeemed spirit shall be suitable to its future heavenly abode.

3. A third difficulty has still to be met. If, at the resurrection, the body is to be so different from what it is at present, will it be *our* body? Shall we when clothed with it be the same persons that we are now? Shall our personal identity be preserved? This question is perhaps not met so fully as the two already considered, because the answer is implied in the whole course of the argument. Yet it would seem to be distinctly in the Apostle's mind, and his view upon the point comes out more particularly in ver. 38. Speaking there of the springing seed, he says, "But God giveth it a body even as it pleased Him, and to each seed a body of its own." According to the later reading, there is no article before ἴδιον σῶμα; and its absence makes a difference in the sense. Τὸ ἴδιον σῶμα would mean a body distinct from other bodies, just as the plant which springs from a grain of wheat is distinct from that which springs from a grain of barley. The emphasis would thus be laid on the fact already considered, that God has such an infinite variety of bodies at His command, that He can have no difficulty in providing His people at the resurrection with the bodies which they may require, and which shall be suitable to their new sphere of life. Ἴδιον σῶμα, without the article, means that God does not

merely make, as it were, a draft upon universal matter in order to find a body for the risen believer, but that He gives him a body of which it can be said, "That is his own body: it corresponds to what *he* is;" and inasmuch as he rises the same man as he died (otherwise we need not speak of a resurrection), it corresponds to what he *was* when he lived on earth. Emphasis is thus laid upon a new fact. The plant which springs from a grain of wheat is not only distinct from that which springs from a grain of barley, it corresponds to what the grain of wheat in itself was. How, or in what particulars, the correspondence is to be traced, the Apostle does not say. He could not. Put a plant of wheat and one of barley along with a grain of wheat and one of barley into the hands of one wholly devoid of experience in these matters, and he certainly could not tell us which of the plants belong to either grain. Even with experience he can only say, "The one plant belongs to the one grain, the other to the other." There is a correspondence between each pair, so that the grain of wheat could have given rise to no plant but the one, the grain of barley to no plant but the other. The grain of wheat has passed into the plant of wheat, the grain of barley into the plant of barley. Identity is preserved through all the changes which the grains have severally undergone.

What has now been said is still further brought out by the contrast of tenses used by the Apostle in ver. 38, "God giveth" (δίδωσιν), the present, "even as it pleased Him" (καθὼς ἠθέλησεν), the definite historic past. Why not "God giveth even as it pleaseth Him"? Because then we should see no law regulating His procedure. He might still indeed bestow a body in such a way as to preserve the identity which is so important; but we might not see that, in doing so, He acted upon a fixed principle. We should be unable to resist the fear that He might choose at one moment one form of body for the plant rising from one kind of seed, and then again another form of body for the same plant. He does not however act thus. He acts upon a law which He has laid down for Himself. It is His eternal will that, through whatever changes the seed or the germ of life passes, there shall be something that connects its latest with its earliest stage.[1]

Nor does the doctrine of the transmutation of species affect the argument. It has been said that it weakens the analogy. "It does not destroy it altogether, because the transmutation, if it occurs at all, is brought about too slowly to be perceptible to the eye. We see only wheat springing from a grain of wheat; and this is enough for the Apostle's purpose.

---

[1] "The καθὼς ἠθέλησεν, pointing back to the time when at His bidding the earth brought forth the 'herb yielding seed after his kind' (Gen. i. 12), and when each seed and the body into which it was to develop were bound by creative wisdom in enduring organic unity" (Ellicott *in loc.*). Comp. also Edwards *in loc.*: "The aorist denotes the first act of God's will determining the constitution of nature. The present expresses the necessary activity of God in the production of every single growth."

The analogy is not the proof."[1] The remark appears to be only so far, not wholly, just. Whatever measure of apparent transmutation of species there may be, it is always within certain lines which fix down the final form of the transmutation to one particular beginning, and not another. The slowness of transmutation too, although in insect life it is often exceedingly rapid, is nothing to the purpose. It is the keeping of the same lines, so that there shall always in the last be something of the first, that is the Apostle's point; and the principle of the Creator's government laid down in the words, "to each seed a body of its own," at once disposes, by analogy, of the difficulty with which he deals.

Changes indeed as great as those here referred to go on continually in the case of man, while we yet remain conscious that we are the same persons that we were. The observation need hardly be repeated, that the particles of our bodies undergo a complete change in the course of a comparatively small number of years. It is of more consequence to notice that the particles lost by us have already entered, or will certainly soon enter, into the bodies of other men whose individuality is as distinct as ours. Yet neither our identity nor that of these others is thereby affected. The very thing which we are apt to think cannot happen has already happened. Transferences not less marvellous than those which are to take place at our death have already taken place with all of us, and are at this moment continually going on in that seething

[1] Edwards *in loc.*

state of existence in which we are all giving and receiving with every breath of air we draw. Disorganization, in a certain sense death, has been long ere now at work in each of us. Others are living by means of what we were. We are living by means of what others were; and yet we live and they live our own independent lives. The memories and experiences of the past were not attached to the particles of our bodies that have disappeared or, in other words, died. They are ours and ours alone, and by no possibility can they become the property of others. If they—that is, if we—do not survive disorganization, death; if we do not survive identical in our personality with what we were, then something as real as the particles of matter has been annihilated; and such a conclusion science contradicts.

Thus then, up to this point, has St. Paul met by analogy the difficulties with which he deals. He has not indeed exhausted his subject. He has much that is positive as well as negative to say. But he has shown "the foolish one," the unobservant student of nature who, consciously or unconsciously, draws his conclusions from what he believes of nature, that he has not studied nature with sufficient care. It may be perfectly true that nature affords no example of individual resurrection in the sense in which we speak of the resurrection of the believer,

> So careful of the type she seems,
> So careless of the single life.

But St. Paul will not go to nature for his proof of that

momentous fact. He will only show that there are processes and laws at work in her which do not contradict it, which may even prepare us for it if it rest upon other sufficient grounds. In the meantime he only dispels the idea that our resurrection bodies either need or will be the same as our present bodies; that they cannot be bodies at all if they are adapted to a heavenly, not an earthly, world; and that the changes we are to undergo must forbid our being hereafter essentially the same personalities that we are now.

Having accomplished this, St. Paul is free—free from having to deal with doubts or to answer difficulties. He is free to spring exultant from the earth, and to expatiate in that glorious realm of hope which is associated with the thought of his risen and exalted Lord.

"So also is the resurrection of the dead. It is sown in corruption; it is raised in incorruption: it is sown in dishonour; it is raised in glory: it is sown in weakness; it is raised in power: it is sown a natural body; it is raised a spiritual body. If there is a natural body, there is also a spiritual body."—1 Cor. xv. 42-44. [R.V.]

Chapter viii.

BY the help of analogies from nature the Apostle has been able to meet three difficulties attending the belief that there is a resurrection of the dead. The dead rise, he had said; and it followed that, so rising, they must have bodies, for without a body no man can be thought of as existing. The first difficulty therefore had been, With what kind of body do the dead come? How can they be thought of as having bodies at all, when the bodies which they possessed during the life in which we knew them have returned to corruption? If they have bodies, had been the second difficulty, will these bodies be adapted to the condition of a heavenly world? If they will be so adapted, had been the third difficulty, and thus be so different from what they were, can personal identity have been preserved? These three questions have been answered, and the application has now to be made in a more positive treatment of the subject.

This application is made at ver. 42: " So also is the resurrection of the dead;" that is, the resurrection of the dead follows the same order and law as may be seen in the analogies of nature that have been spoken of. We have here one of those instances of breviloquence which are common in all languages, a thought implied though not fully expressed. In speaking of the plant which sprang from the seed, St. Paul evidently did not think of the mere fact of the springing alluded to. He thought also of the plant itself as a living plant, and of the new state into which it was introduced. He thought of the life that was in the new form, and of which the new form was the expression. In like manner he does not think now only of the *act* of rising from the dead, but of the *life* which follows it. Something of a similar kind, although there the tense of the verb used makes the meaning clearer, is to be found in ver. 4 of this chapter: "And that He (Christ) hath been raised [not 'was raised' of Authorized Version] on the third day." Not merely did Christ rise, but His Resurrection was to ever-enduring, eternal life.

If what has been said be admitted, it may help us over a difficulty connected with the next following words, rendered in both the Authorized and Revised Versions, "It is sown in corruption," etc. The subject spoken of, it is said, is the body, which indeed is expressly named in ver. 44: σπείρεται σῶμα ψυχικόν. Σῶμα is therefore to be taken back to the beginning of ver. 42, and the "it" of the English rendering is to be understood as "the body." So most commentators. But there are difficulties in the way of accepting this view; for (1) Although the Apostle has

CHAP. VIII THE RESURRECTION OF THE DEAD   141

been treating of the body, it is less the body alone than the body regarded as the outward organ and expression of the man that he has in his eye; (2) The σῶμα of ver. 44 is too far off, and we ought to find it mentioned in ver. 42. Even when it first meets us in verse 44, it is a predicate, rather than directly the subject of the sentence; (3) If supplied as proposed, we shall hardly be able to avoid thinking of death and burial as the moment at which the sowing takes place, and not a few commentators who advocate its introduction as *subject* at the beginning of ver. 42 allow that this cannot be done.[1] Another rendering accordingly has been suggested, in which σπείρεται is treated as an impersonal verb.[2] "It is sown;" that is, "There is a sowing in corruption," etc. The point need not be enlarged on; for, on the one hand, a reference to the body cannot be denied; and, on the other hand, there is a sufficiently general admission that the Apostle must be understood to speak of the body, not at the instant only when it is buried, but as the habitation of man during his present earthly life. When, in the first clause of ver. 42, he says, "So also is the resurrection of the dead," he has in view, not simply the act of rising, but the resurrection state into which believers enter. In like manner, when he speaks of the νεκροί, though the immediate reference is to their death, he is really thinking of their whole mortal in contrast with their whole immortal life. All

[1] Comp. Ellicott, Edwards.
[2] Comp. Moulton's *Winer*, p. 656; Hofmann *in loc.*; Godet *in loc.*

the earthly course of man, from its beginning to its end, from the cradle to the grave, is the time of his being sown; and truth is that

> Which we are toiling all our lives to find,
> In darkness lost, the darkness of the grave.

No other interpretation does justice to the context. The terms "dishonour" and "weakness" are too wide to find a suitable application to the body only when it is committed to the dust; while it would be extremely unnatural to call it a σῶμα ψυχικόν, a body with a sensuous life, at the very time when that life has left it.

Thus then, contrasting the life of man in his earthly body with his life in his resurrection body, St. Paul proceeds to point out how infinitely more glorious is the latter than the former. "It is sown in corruption; it is raised in incorruption: it is sown in dishonour; it is raised in glory: it is sown in weakness; it is raised in power: it is sown a natural body; it is raised a spiritual body." What is the meaning of these appellations?

Godet, adopting the right reference of the sowing, not to the act of burial, but to all the earthly life of man, supposes that, in the terms thus used, the Apostle travels backwards in thought through the different stages of a mortal pilgrimage from death to birth. "Corruption" thus refers to death and dissolution in the grave; "dishonour" to all the ills and miseries which precede and prepare the way for death; "weakness," to the helplessness of infancy when the child is born; while the word "natural" ($\psi \upsilon \chi \iota \kappa \acute{o} \varsigma$) carries us still further back to the instant at which the breath of life is communicated to the physical germ about to be developed into the instrument and organism of the future life on earth. The explanation can hardly be looked at in any other light than as fanciful and unnatural. Had the Apostle been alluding to the different stages of man's earthly life, he would surely have begun at the beginning, and have passed onward to the end. But there is no need to think of stages. Each term used is applicable to human life as a whole, and the progress lying latent in the words is one, not of time, but of thought.

Thus the glorified body which man is to possess at his resurrection and in his resurrection state rises before the mind of the Apostle "in corruption"; and he exclaims, "It is sown in corruption; it is raised in incorruption." He has no thought of sin in saying so, but only of liability to change and to dissolution. Here all things pass away. Years, as they sweep over us, and especially when they bring us near the great step which transfers us to the eternal world, bring with them only increasing infirmities, more multiplied tokens that the tabernacle in which we dwell shall soon be altogether taken down. There, "incorruption:" no insidious approaches of sickness or disease, no colour fading from the cheek or light from the eye, no wearied frame hardly able to bear the burden of itself, no palsied limb but the blessed glow of health and strength diffused through the whole man, and to be enhanced rather than diminished as the ages of eternity run on. Next, "in glory:" "It is sown in dishonour; it is raised in glory." Again the Apostle has no thought of any positive dishonour inflicted by either God or man upon the body during the present life; and surely still less does he think of any later contempt poured upon the thought of it, as if it were supposed to lie in the grave unremembered and unloved. "Dishonour" is simply in contrast with "glory." Twice in other passages of his writings does St. Paul use the word, when he would express the nature of those meaner vessels of a great house, which are either made of wood or stone, instead of gold or silver, or which, if made of the same material as others, are less elaborately finished and adorned.[1] The true parallel to the thought is to be found in the contrast presented to us in the Epistle to the Philippians between the body of our humiliation which is to be fashioned anew, and the body of Christ's glory to which it is to be conformed. Such is the lowliness of man's body now. Fearfully and wonderfully as it is made, it is yet a poor frame in comparison with what it shall be when "the righteous shall shine forth as the sun in the kingdom of their Father," and when they shall be clothed with a glory corresponding to that of the "new heavens and the new earth wherein dwelleth righteousness." Once more, St. Paul sees the

[1] Rom. ix. 21; 2 Tim. ii. 20.

body of man in "power:" "It is sown in weakness; it is raised in power." Here it is frail, helpless, exposed to infirmities and diseases of all kinds. There it is possessed of power, and has gained a complete mastery over every ill.

In all this, as especially appears from the words that follow, and have still to be considered, the Apostle is not thinking of the effect produced upon man's earthly state by his fall from the condition in which he was originally created. He has in view a state of matters which existed previously to the fall. No doubt there is a sense in which it may be said that sin has brought into the world "death and all our woe." But it seems to be the clear teaching of St. Paul throughout the passage now under consideration, that the "corruption," the "dishonour," and the "weakness" of which he speaks are properties of our present human frame in itself, properties that belonged even to the frame of our first parents in their state in paradise. No ethical idea therefore is to be attached to the words. Man, even in his best estate, had been fitted for life in this earthly, material scene, in which he was to work out and to pass through his preparation for a higher. That higher scene now shines brightly before the eye of the Apostle, as he places himself on the other side of the river of time and death; and it is one of "incorruption," of "glory," and of "power."

At ver. 44 of the chapter St. Paul continues his description of the contrast between the present and the resurrection state of believers, yet with an important change in his line of thought. Hitherto he had spoken of the contrast in its more outward features, and the arrangement thus indicated might have been nothing more than an arbitrary arrangement on the part of God. Without regard to any deeper principles of His government, God might have simply willed that the change to take effect on the bodies of His saints at the resurrection should be from corruption to incorruption, from dishonour to glory, from weakness to power. At the point of the argument which we now reach new ground is occupied, and the nature of the body to be bestowed upon believers when they arise from the dead is brought into connexion with everlasting principles of the divine administration of the universe.

1. The fact meets us. "It is sown a natural body; it is raised a spiritual body." The words here used, "natural" (accepting that translation in the meantime), "spiritual," and "body," cannot be examined in a paper such as this with that fulness of statement which their importance might justify or might even seem to demand, but a few remarks upon them must be made.

(1) What is the conception to be attached to the word "body"? Certainly not that commonly entertained, that it is the mere covering of the soul, standing to the soul in a relation similar to that of the shell to the kernel of a nut. The connexion between the two is much more intimate. The body

CHAP. VIII   THE RESURRECTION OF THE DEAD   147

is an organism, and its organized existence depends, alike in its beginning and in its continuance, upon the fact that a vital power not only dwells in it as in a house, but permeates or interpenetrates it in such a way that all its different parts or members constitute one whole (1 Cor. xii. 12-26). From the head "all the body fitly framed and knit together through every joint of the supply, according to the working in due measure of each several part, maketh the increase of the body" (Eph. iv. 16). This vital power however may be of entirely different kinds. It may be spiritual or carnal, heavenly or earthly. There is no closer connexion between the body as such and any one of the forces by which it may be animated and used, than between the body and any other of these forces. The σῶμα (body) is not the σάρξ (flesh). The latter may be the ruling principle in the former, and may become so identified with it that when the σῶμα is spoken of, it may, as in Romans viii. 10, include the σάρξ. But the σάρξ has no necessary relation to the σῶμα. Its power may be destroyed while the σῶμα still remains the σῶμα, employed as their instruments by good instead of evil principles. Hence, accordingly, the σῶμα may be "holy," which the σάρξ can never be; it is "for the Lord, and the Lord is for it" (1 Cor. vi. 13); "it is even the 'temple'— the ναός, the innermost shrine—of the Holy Spirit in believers" (1 Cor. vi. 19): it is to be presented to God "a living sacrifice, holy, acceptable to God, our reasonable or spiritual (Revised Version, margin) service" (Rom. xii. 1): nay, it was the instrument fashioned by the Almighty for the eternal Son, that by means of it He might complete the work of man's redemption (Heb. x. 5).

The idea therefore apt to be entertained by many, that there is an incompatibility, or even a contrariety, between what is spiritual and what is bodily, is wholly false. In St. Paul's view there is no such opposition. With him spiritual is opposed to what is either carnal or belonging to the same category, and the distinguishing feature of what is called the "body" is, not that it is better fitted for what is evil than for what is good, but that it is the form in which either the one or the other is made manifest.

Again, we are nowhere taught that the particles of which the body is composed are necessarily heavy and sluggish, ill adapted to the activity and life of the spirit. For aught we know they may be of an entirely different description. Not their weight, but their relation to one another, their dependence upon one another, their interest in one another, and their mutual helpfulness, constitute them a "body." The use of that word throws no light upon the nature of the particles of which the body is composed, either in its earthly or its heavenly, its pre-resurrection or its post-resurrection, state. These particles may be like those of our present frames, or they may be in striking contrast with them. The word "body" only says that there shall be an investiture or framework within which the vital force shall dwell, and by which each possessor of a body shall be separated from his fellows.

(2) " Natural " ($\psi\nu\chi\iota\kappa\acute{o}\varsigma$). The translation is that of both the Authorized and Revised Versions, but few will be found to deny that it is not a happy one. For, in the first place, the word " natural " is in a high degree ambiguous; and in the second place, it conveys no conception of any internal force or power in man which expresses itself in the particular kind of body spoken of. Yet the term of the original is exceedingly difficult to translate. It is not of frequent occurrence in the New Testament. Except in the verses immediately before us, it is found only three times in the whole compass of that book: in 1 Corinthians ii. 14, James iii. 15, and Jude 19. In the first of these passages it is again rendered, alike in the Authorized Version and the Revised Version, " natural," and in the second and third " sensual ; " although the revisers sufficiently indicate their perplexity by attaching to it on these last occasions a double margin, " natural " or " animal."

There may be no complete remedy for this, as no word of the English language properly represents the Greek. Certainly the refuges of despair suggested by recent inquirers, " soulish " and " soulual," are still more objectionable. Yet, even allowing this, it is hardly possible not to feel that each of the three renderings found in the Revised Version and its margin leads us astray. The adjective, it will be admitted, must be understood in the sense of the substantive from which it comes, and ψυχή means neither what is "natural," nor what is "sensual," nor what is "animal" in human nature. ψυχή is the life-principle, the principle of personality, in man regarded simply as a creature of this present world, and in contradistinction to the religious principle which connects him with another and a higher world. It is not necessarily sinful, although it is capable of admitting a sinful as well as, in other circumstances, a Divine principle to rule in it. And it is not necessarily a degraded thing, for it may include our highest gifts of reason, intelligence, and emotion, so long as these are unconnected with a spiritual world. The essence, in short, of the biblical conception of ψυχή appears to be that it is that in man which adapts him to this world of sense in which he for the present moves; that which, along with the body, constitutes him a part of the visible and tangible creation.

These considerations at once suggest the true meaning to be assigned to the word ψυχικός, neither "natural," nor "sensual," nor "animal," but ruled by the senses, or by the material things around us as they are apprehended by the senses; and the English adjective which appears to come nearest to the expression of this thought is "sensuous." It will be found upon examination that this rendering is admirably adapted to the three passages above referred to. The last of the three indeed, Jude 19, demands it. To read "sensual, having not the Spirit," is to introduce a contrast of an unscriptural and most misleading kind. In the meantime therefore, contenting ourselves simply with translating the word, what we read of man's present state, and especially of his bodily organization during his present state is, "it is sown a sensuous body."

(3) "Spiritual." There can be little or no doubt as to the meaning of this word. It stands in a relation to spirit similar to that in which "sensuous" stands to sense; and the word "spirit," when spoken of man, points to that part of human nature which brings us into contact with God. "God is spirit" (John iv. 24), and there must therefore be something in man, come whence it may, and either at the first or later, which enables us to hold communion with spirit, and partakes of the nature of spirit. Such is the teaching of the New Testament. There is another side of human nature than that which is alone appealed to by the things of sense. There is the spiritual side, that by which thought and aspiration pass from the material to the immaterial, from the visible to the invisible, from the earthly to the super-earthly, from man to God. And this spiritual principle, for the complete appropriation of which man is originally fitted, may become the dominating principle of the man, and therefore of the body with which man works. That is the spiritual in man.

Thus then we are prepared to follow the contrast between man's present and future state, as, in the first place, the facts of that contrast are set before us in the words, "It is sown a sensuous body; it is raised a spiritual body." The body now possessed by man is, above all, distinguished by this, that it is linked to the objects of sense and governed by their influence. Not indeed that such a state is in itself necessarily low and degraded, one of which we can speak only with opprobrium or contempt. We may justly use far other language; for how striking and illustrative of Divine wisdom is the correspondence between each of our senses and the particular department of external nature to which it is adapted. How are our faculties called into exercise, strengthened, and delighted by the appeals continually made to them through the objects of earth and sky! How are our affections nourished by the various relationships in which we stand to one another in the family, in society, in the nation, in the world at large!

> What a piece of work is a man! how noble in reason! how infinite in faculties! in form and moving how express and admirable! in action how like an angel! in apprehension how like a god! the beauty of the world! the paragon of animals!

And the body is scarcely less an instrument in all this than the mind and heart. Let us not condemn the "sensuous body." It is "fearfully and wonderfully made."

In one respect indeed such a body fails. It is not completely adapted to that spiritual and eternal world, relation to which is as truly a part of what God has designed for us as is relation to the world of sense. To the spiritual world it is not adapted, for how limited is the body when it comes to deal with the unseen! To the eternal it is not adapted, for how brief is the span of its existence before it returns to the dust! Nay, the loftier the flight of the spirit in its religious life, the sooner does the body feel itself unable to bear it longer; and, though "the hoary head is a crown of glory when it is found in the way of righteousness," yet old age has already one foot in the grave, and the other may have to follow it at the very moment when the life seemed to be most full of instruction and most rich in promise. The "sensuous body" has at best its elements of "corruption" and "dishonour" and "weakness;" and, unless there be another principle stronger than they, they must prevail at last.

Such a principle, accordingly, the Apostle tells us that there is, as he points us forward to the time when what has been sown a sensuous body shall be "raised a spiritual body." As the "sensuous body" is the body ruled by sense, so the "spiritual body" is the body ruled by spirit. We have already seen that that time has not yet come: but it will come, when the limits of the sensuous world shall no longer hem us in; when the restraints of our earthly, material investiture shall be broken through; and when, under the all-pervading and dominating power of spirit, the body, in its strength, rapidity of movement, and ever-renewed youthfulness of vigour, shall be the meet companion of the soul in its loftiest flights. In the spiritual body the restrictions of the sensuous body shall wholly disappear. With it the believer shall rise superior to languor and weariness and death. Then shall be said of him literally what now can be said of him only ideally, that he is fitted for serving God day and night in His temple, and for walking with Him in the land, the sun of which no more goes down, and the moon of which no more withdraws itself.

Of both the kinds of body thus referred to we have undoubted examples in the life of our Lord. While He tabernacled among men He had a "sensuous" body, like the other members of that family in which He was taking the place of elder brother. He hungered; He thirsted; He sat weary by Jacob's well; He fell asleep, probably worn out by fatigue, in the boat upon the Sea of Galilee; during His agony in the garden His sweat was like great drops of blood falling down to the ground. "Since then the children are sharers in blood and flesh, He also himself in like manner partook of the same" (Heb. ii. 14). After His Resurrection there was a great change. We read no longer of hunger, or thirst, or weariness, or pores of the body opened by pain and agony. We read of a body which was obviously altogether different from what it had been, but was in every respect obedient and subservient to the spirit. In that body in its two different stages we behold the type and model of our own, as it is and as it is destined to be. The experience of the

Head shall also be the experience of the members. "It is sown a sensuous body; it is raised a spiritual body."

We have looked at the facts as stated by the Apostle, but the most remarkable part of this 44th verse is—

2. The principle to which St. Paul refers in illustration and confirmation of his statement. According to the reading of the Textus Receptus indeed—the reading followed in the Authorized Version — the Apostle simply goes on to say, "There is a sensuous body, and there is a spiritual body;" but the reading adopted by the most distinguished later editors of the New Testament, and resting upon what seems an overpowering weight of evidence, supplies the translation adopted in the Revised Version: "If there is a sensuous (in Revised Version 'natural') body, there is also a spiritual body." The fact that the one exists leads to the conclusion that the other also exists, or that it will in due time do so. Upon what fundamental principle, or upon what process of reasoning, does this conclusion rest? Hardly upon the conviction only that the spiritual body is "the perfect development" of the sensuous body, and that the existence of the latter, with its great capabilities, "suggests and, to a mind that believes in the living and good God, demonstrates the future existence of the former. The resurrection of the dead is an instance of the universal law of progress."[1] This may be in part the explanation.

[1] Edwards, *in loc.*: comp. Beet, *in loc.*

St. Paul certainly seems, throughout this passage as a whole, to imply, that there is a great law of progress in the universe, and it may be that he found an instance of it in the fact that the sensuous body will at last pass into the spiritual body. But that is not his thought at the present moment; and, in so far as it involves the idea of a *gradual* development, it is rather opposed to his convictions than expressive of them. His reasoning appears rather to rest upon the principle that, when God gives the inward, He gives also its appropriate outward garb or frame; that He gives that, in short, without which we should only have an idea in the Divine Mind. Whatever be the human life-force, St. Paul believes that it will have a suitable vehicle for its energies.

Now two things he knew, and we may know. First, he knew, as a matter of daily experience, that the law upon the thought of which he was dwelling was exemplified in our sensuous life. The life-force ruling us in that life had a sensuous frame adapted to it. Secondly, he knew that there was such a thing as the spirit-life, both in Christ and in the members of His body. He had already written, and was to write more, to the Corinthian Church about that spirit-life. He and they knew it in Christ. They believed in the risen Lord as "Spirit" (1 Cor. vi. 17). They were yet again to be taught the same lesson, and, in addition, that they were to be "transformed into the same image from glory to glory, even as from the Lord the Spirit" (2 Cor. iii. 18). Unless therefore they denied the higher spirit-life and the risen Lord, it followed that, as the sensuous life has now its appropriate earthly frame so the spirit-life must some day receive its corresponding spiritual frame. St. Paul's mind had been already full of a similar thought at ver. 38, when he spoke of the manner in which the vital force of the seed, stirred into action by being committed to the soil, received from God a new body, as it pleased Him. The same thought, although in a more general form, occupies him now; and it is the sole thought upon which he dwells. He says nothing of any innate power possessed by the spirit to weave, as it were, for itself a corresponding covering; nor does he enter into the question whether the embodiment is produced by an instantaneous fiat of the Creator, or by a long and gradual process, in the course of which the nobler vital principle overcomes irregularities, smooths away roughnesses, and by imperceptible degrees establishes perfect harmony between the inner life and the outward form. He deals as yet simply with the fact that, as there is a spiritual principle in believers which will one day assert in them complete dominion, so we may be assured that to that principle there will yet be given its corresponding framework. It had been thus with Christ, whose heavenly life, led even now at the right hand of the Father, was acknowledged by all Christians at Corinth to have found expression in His heavenly body. Could it be otherwise with those who followed in His footsteps and were partakers of His spirit? No; for that heavenly or spiritual body had not been a mere gift to the risen Lord, in return for all that He had done and suffered. It had been bestowed upon Him in fulfilment of a universal law; and, if that law took effect upon the Head, it would in due time, as the members shared the spirit of the Head, take effect also upon them.

"So also it is written, The first man Adam became a living soul. The last Adam became a life-giving spirit. Howbeit that is not first which is spiritual, but that which is natural; then that which is spiritual."—1 COR. xv. 45, 46. [R.V.]

Chapter ix.

AT the close of the verse immediately preceding the point now reached by us, St. Paul had laid it down as a settled and incontrovertible principle, that, "If there is a natural (or, rather, sensuous) body, there is also a spiritual body." The words present all the appearance of having been regarded by the Apostle as an axiom. They rest upon the conception which universal experience compels us to attach to men whenever we think of them as living beings, that is, whenever we think of them in the only light in which they are a matter of concern to us. As living beings we know them, care for them, and must reason about them. But this living being of theirs, as known to us, consists of two things, a life-force and a body in which the life-force dwells. Extinguish the one, and you have nothing but a dead framework hastening to corruption. Extinguish the other, and you have but a shadowy phantom, not a man. When therefore we have the one, we may rest assured that God, who will not leave His creatures hopelessly stunted and imperfect, will add the other. But there are two wholly different life-forces or inner states of man,—one connecting him with the visible, tangible, material world ; the other connecting him with God and the spiritual, invisible, and heavenly world. That both exist is indisputable. No one will deny that the lower life-force is a reality. Evidence is borne to it at every step taken, and through every act performed, by men in the material sphere around them. Is the higher life-force less a reality than the lower ? Let us remember that St. Paul is speaking to Christians, and he knows the answer that they will and must give. He would have given it himself. When he exclaims in writing to the Galatians, " I have been crucified with Christ; yet I live; and yet no longer I, but Christ liveth in me: and that life which I now live in the flesh I live in faith, the faith which is in the Son of God, who loved me, and gave Himself for me ; " or when again, in writing to the Philippians, he says, " For to me to live is Christ, and to die is gain " (Gal. ii. 20 ; Phil. i. 21),—upon what is he dwelling ? Not on outward proof only, or evidence presented to the senses. He had had outward proof of the *facts* which lay at the bottom of his spiritual life, and in many passages of his speeches and writings he shows his dependence upon it, and his joy in the thought that it was so satisfactory and complete. But no proof of a similar kind could bear witness to the reality of his inner life, that life of which he says, " It was the good pleasure of God, who separated me, even from my mother's womb, and called me through His grace, to reveal His Son in me " (Gal. i. 15, 16). The evidence of such a life depended upon his own experience of it. The Spirit of Christ living in him brought conviction to the Apostle's mind; and to any one who would have denounced this as enthusiasm or self-delusion he would simply have replied, "I know in whom I have believed." The answer that he would himself have given he is well assured will be given by Christian men everywhere.

But if all Christians would give that answer, how much more even those to whom he was now writing ! They were part of the Church of Christ in Corinth ; and there was no city of the time in which greater or more undeniable evidence had been afforded to its Christian inhabitants of the reality of the higher life which animated them. They knew that, beyond the limits of earth, their Redeemer ruled in spiritual power and with a body glorified. All Christians, wherever their lot was cast, possessed that knowledge. In addition to that, it was known at Corinth, to a degree to which it seems to have been known nowhere else in that age, that the glorified Lord communicated His Spirit to His people. In what high terms does the Apostle, in the beginning of this very epistle, describe the state of Christians there ! " I thank my God always concerning you, for the grace of God which was given you in Christ Jesus ; that in everything ye were enriched in Him, in all utterance and all knowledge, . . . so that ye come behind in no gift " (chap. i. 4-7) ; and at a later point in the same epistle what a splendid exuberance of gifts does he describe them as possessing : " the word of wisdom," "the word of knowledge," "faith," "gifts of healings," "workings of miracles," "prophecy," "discernings of spirits," "divers kinds of tongues," "the interpretation of tongues;" and all these were wrought in them by "the one and the same Spirit, dividing to each one severally even as He will!" (chap. xii. 8-11). Who could doubt the reality of the Spirit-life, of the Spirit-force, alike in their Saviour and in themselves? Therein lies one of the points of deepest interest in St. Paul's argument. He takes for granted that spiritual experience is a fact, and he reasons upon it. He is not afraid of being met with a charge on the part of some sceptic, that he is begging the question, and that the reality of the Spirit and of the Spirit-life must first be proved. There is no further proof needed he, as it were, exclaims. Where the Spirit is He shows that He is, and he who has received Him becomes as conscious of His power as of breathing the air around him. The Church of Christ has felt, and still feels, this too little. She talks of proofs, of evidences, as if they were not less convincing than the Multiplication Table. She would often produce more effect were she to give the Spirit first and the proof afterwards. At any rate it was certain that there was a life of the Spirit as well as a life of sense. The argument is thus clear. God has clothed our lower life-force with a sensuous body adapted to it, and we may be sure that He will also clothe our higher life-force with the spiritual body which will alone be its fitting habitation.

The fact of man's existence in a sensuous body is thus the *primary* thought in St. Paul's mind; and this may help to explain one of the difficulties often felt in connexion with the quotation from the book of Genesis contained in the next following words. That quotation unquestionably ends with the word "soul" in the clause, "The first man Adam became a living soul;" and it is meant to end there. No other idea ought ever to have been entertained. Even on the ground of St. Paul's knowledge of Scripture, it ought never to have been supposed that he intended the last clause of ver. 45 to be regarded as a part of his quotation. But, apart from that, the words would not have proved his immediate point, the existence of the sensuous body as something included in the Divine plan. That is the premiss from which he reasons to the existence of a spiritual body; and that therefore is all that he would establish by Scripture.

Besides this, however, it may be observed, that the latter half of ver. 45 not only was not, it could not be in Scripture, or at least in any Scripture that might be thought of here. As we have yet to see more fully, the point of time to which it relates did not arrive till centuries after the canon of the Old Testament Scriptures had been closed. To imagine therefore, that St. Paul thought of quoting the words, "The last Adam became a life-giving spirit," as words of Scripture, is to attribute to him both an ignorance with which he could not possibly be chargeable, and a credulity as to the ease with which his readers might be misled that is equally incredible. The direct line of thought is simply this: the first man, a creature of earthly sensations, had a sensuous body. The inference is, the last man, being spirit, was also lifegiving; and as there can be no life without a body adapted to it, the purpose or plan of God must include a spiritual as well as a sensuous body.

The Apostle's appeal, then, is to Scripture. Why? Because Scripture is the expression of God's plan. In vers. 3 and 4 of this chapter, a similar appeal is made for a similar purpose. Christ is there said to have died for our sins "according to the Scriptures," and to have been raised again "according to the Scriptures." Not that in either instance any mere prophecy is fulfilled, or any mere fact of history recorded upon the Divine authority. The meaning is, that Scripture contains the mind and purpose of the Almighty. Does it tell us that man at his creation was a being possessed of a vital force clothed in a sensuous body? We may infer that this was part of a scheme or plan, which, having been fulfilled, as we see, in one part, will in due season be fulfilled in all its parts.

On the slight changes made in the form of the quotation it is not necessary to dwell; yet they are not without a bearing on St. Paul's line of thought, and they thus help us to understand more clearly what that is. As the words occur in Genesis ii. 7 in the LXX., from which they are taken, they contain no πρῶτος and no 'Αδάμ, running simply ἐγένετο ὁ ἄνθρωπος εἰς ψυχὴν ζῶσαν (the man became a living soul). But St. Paul was justified in inserting πρῶτος (first), because there could be no doubt that the person referred to was really the first man, the words of Genesis immediately preceding the quoted statement being, "And God formed man of the dust of the ground, and breathed into his nostrils the breath of life." He was also justified in inserting Ἀδάμ, because that man was Adam. As, accordingly, the words, "The last Adam became a life-giving spirit," are already at the beginning of the verse in St. Paul's thoughts, the insertion of the words "first" and "Adam" in the quotation need not occasion the slightest difficulty. At the same time, the fact that the words are inserted is highly instructive. Keeping them in view, we see more clearly than we might otherwise have done what is passing through the Apostle's mind, and we are led by them to certain ideas of his which must be taken into account if we would understand him fully. The first of these ideas lurks in the word "Adam," the double use of which shows us, what need only be hinted at now (it will meet us again), that St. Paul is thinking of two heads of two lines of descendants, who convey to those that spring from them what they themselves are. The second idea appears in the word "first" when combined with the word "last" in the sense in which it is here used. That sense is precisely similar to the sense in which any one examining the passage will find it necessary to understand the adverbial "last" (ἔσχατον) in ver. 8 of this chapter: "And last of all He appeared to me also." In neither case does "last" mean simply the last of a series who has appeared but may be followed by another. It means the last absolutely, the last of the series to which the person or the thing spoken of belongs, to be followed by no other. St Paul does not merely say that there was an Adam who had appeared as the first man, and that then there was another Adam who had appeared later, and who might still have a successor. He sees that in God's plan there are two heads in the human family, *and no more*. The one, it is true, is the head of the whole family; the other is the head of believers only. But the point is, that the last come is also in such a sense the last to come, and that our position in God's plan must be regulated by our relation either to Him or to the one who went before Him. Nor is it any objection to this that in ver. 47 the Apostle uses the word "second" instead of the word "last." He does so because there will then be a change of thought, because he will then be tracing the *historical* unfolding of the Divine economy as it is evolved, first, in a first Adam, and, secondly, in a second. At present it is not so much a historical unfolding of the economy that he has in view. He would grasp its principles; and for this purpose all its parts must be embraced in one whole, from its beginning to its end, from its first to its last. The words "first" and "Adam" added to the quotation are thus by no means unimportant. They belong directly to the current of thought, and are cast up by it.

A third word here before us calls also for a moment's notice—"life-giving." Why not simply "living"? Would not "living spirit" have been a closer parallel and contrast to "living soul"? It would be so could "spirit" simply live its own life, and be therewith satisfied. But spirit cannot thus live. The conception of something that merely lives, that exerts no quickening power on others, is not enough for πνεῦμα. In its very nature spirit is life-giving. It is the water of which Jesus spoke to the woman of Samaria, "The water that I shall give him shall become in him a fountain of springing water (not a well of stagnant water, however deep and full), unto eternal life" (John iv. 14). Therefore must the last Adam, when He became "spirit," have been unable to confine His spirit-existence to Himself. It was necessary that He should be not simply "living," but "life-giving."

Such then are the Apostle's words, and now what is his thought? It is that two great Heads include within them and sum up the history of man. The one is the first, the other is the second Adam: the first, a living soul, sensuous, and all his descendants like him; the second, a life-giving spirit, and all His descendants like Him, spiritual, life-giving spirit. There is no help for it. We must belong either to the one or to the other. To which of the two we ought to belong we shall be told by-and-by.

From these minor particulars we have now to turn

to two questions of the greatest interest connected with the words of this verse. To what points of time does St. Paul refer in its two clauses? When was it that the first Adam became a living soul? When was it that the last Adam became a life-giving spirit?

1. When did the first Adam become a living soul? The answer to this question seems undoubtedly to be, Before the Fall. The passage quoted from Genesis clearly indicates this by its position in that book. It is connected with the first account of the creation of man: "And the Lord God formed man of the dust of the ground, and breathed into his nostrils the breath of life; and man became a living soul" (Gen. ii. 7). The words thus relate to man's primal condition, while yet in his state of innocence. Even then our first parents were not all that the Almighty intended them to be. They were, it is true, endowed with more than a mere animal soul. They were certainly higher than the beasts that perish. They were perfectly adapted to this present world. They had not only their organs of sense, together with appetites, affections, and passions; they had also intelligence, reason, imagination, memory, together with all that might fit them for a thoughtful and, so far as this world goes, an elevated life. Yet, even under his highest aspect, St. Paul would say, man was not fitted for the state of existence to which it was God's design to raise him at a future time. He had a body that was naturally mortal,

that was not dominated by the spirit which is alone above all connexion with the dust, which is alone unchangeable and eternal. Some means, no doubt, might and would have been found by his merciful Creator to save him from that decay and death which belonged to all merely sensuous things. Whether by eating of the tree of life, or in some other way, he would have been raised in the scale of being, and delivered from that penalty of death which was threatened to transgression. But only thus. Notwithstanding the opinion to the contrary entertained by distinguished theologians,[1] nothing seems clearer than that the Apostle is not here thinking of our first parent after the Fall, but in his estate of innocence.

2. When did the last Adam become a life-giving spirit? It has been said, At the Incarnation.[2] But the whole argument of the Apostle makes it necessary to suppose that the Resurrection, and not the Incarnation, of our Lord is in his view. At ver. 21 he had said that "Since through man came death, through man came also the resurrection of the dead;" and that the words do not simply mean through gift of man is proved by the following verse, where we read that "*in* the Christ shall all be made alive." In other words, the meaning is, that as we die in Adam, who died, so in Christ, who was raised from the dead, are we also raised. The thought of Christ risen is the very foundation of the whole reasoning. Again, when,

[1] Comp. Ellicott *in loc.*   [2] Comp. Edwards *in loc.*

at ver. 23, the order of the resurrection is spoken of, it is obviously the Risen Christ who is described as "the first-fruits." And, once more, the words under consideration are introduced as the expression of the fundamental fact upon which the prospect of the resurrection of the dead has been rested in the immediately preceding statement. Besides this, it is to be remembered that the last Adam did not become a *life-giving* Spirit at His Incarnation. He was then made in all things like unto those brethren whom He had come to save. He took upon Him the very nature, with all its frailties and limitations, possessed by them, that He might enter into their condition, and might lead them on in that way of toil and suffering and death by which alone they can reach His Father's kingdom. It is true that our Lord, even during His earthly life, was in possession of the Spirit, and St. Paul's conception of Spirit is, that it always acts towards what is external to it, that it is always in itself "*life-giving*." But herein lay the peculiarity in the case of Christ,—He was *Himself* limited, confined, restrained by the "flesh" which He had assumed; and, inasmuch as in giving His Spirit He gives *Himself*, not merely something else which He has to bestow, it necessarily follows that the Spirit dwelling in Him could not, during the days of His humiliation, exercise that quickening or life-giving power on others which properly belonged to it. Only when the limits occasioned by the "flesh" were broken through could Christ communicate *Himself*, and therefore only then could He communicate His Spirit, with perfect freedom. Thus, although Christ always possessed in Himself a fulness of the life-giving Spirit, He could not *become* that life-giving Spirit to others until, rising from the dead in a glorified body, He threw aside for ever the wrappings of earth by which He had been previously confined.

This teaching of St. Paul is not confined to the passage with which we are now dealing. It lies also at the bottom of such words as these, "But if the Spirit of Him that raised up Jesus from the dead dwelleth in you, He that raised up Christ Jesus from the dead shall quicken also your mortal bodies because of His Spirit that dwelleth in you" (Rom. viii. 11); and it is still more clearly expressed when the same Apostle says, "Now the Lord is the Spirit: and where the Spirit of the Lord is, there is liberty. But we all, with unveiled face reflecting as a mirror the glory of the Lord, are transformed into the same image from glory to glory, even as from the Lord the Spirit" (2 Cor. iii. 17, 18). In both these passages it is the Risen Lord who is before us, and that in His estate of Spirit, in the freedom with which He works in that state, and in the transference to us of a spirit which quickens our mortal bodies into a resurrection like His own.

Only then at His Resurrection, and not at His Incarnation, did our Lord become a life-giving Spirit. Only at His Resurrection was He in the full sense of the words the "last Adam." Then however He did become the Head of a new line of descendants; and the facts recorded in Scripture of the period of His history which followed this point illustrate the truth. It was only after His Resurrection that "He breathed on His disciples, and saith unto them, Receive ye Holy Spirit" (John xx. 22). Only after the same event, on the day of Pentecost, did He shed forth His Spirit on the assembled disciples and inaugurate the entrance of the Christian Church upon her mission (Acts ii.); and only with His Risen life is connected that bestowal of His Spirit upon His people by which they are enabled to bear true witness to Him, and to convict the world of sin and righteousness and judgment (John xv. 26, 27; xvi. 7, 8). All this then He has done and does in the only body in which it is possible for Him to do it, in the glorified body which He now possesses in His heavenly kingdom. The "last Adam" is not simply the incarnate, but the risen and glorified Redeemer.

There is, however, something more to be considered; for the thought might naturally enough occur to many, If there is not only a sensuous, but a spiritual body, and if the spiritual body is, as it must be, so much more glorious than the sensuous body, why might we not have it now? To give an answer to this question seems to be the main object of the following verse, "Howbeit that is not first which is spiritual, but that which is sensuous; then that which is spiritual" (ver. 46).

That the verse begins with ἀλλά is sufficient to

show that we are not to have a mere repetition of what has gone before, but that new matter is to be introduced; and this new matter seems intended to meet the difficulty just mentioned. Not that we have now such a general or abstract statement as that, in the very nature of things, the "sensuous" must precede the "spiritual." The Apostle appears rather to have in view the historical manifestation of God's plan as exhibited in Adam and in Christ. Let us look at them, and in them we shall see what is really the order of the universe, so far at least as it is connected with the thought of time. We then have brought before us in a concrete form the essential relations of things to one another. And, had St. Paul pursued his thought further, he might have added, No wonder that it should be so, for all things must be moulded upon the pattern which has existed from eternity in the Divine Mind. Where then may that pattern be best seen? Surely nowhere so well as in the contrast between the first and the last Adam. The first Adam begins the history of humanity; the last Adam carries it to its consummation. Compare the two with one another, and you will at once learn by the comparison that the sensuous precedes the spiritual, that the limitations of the earthly come before the freedom of the heavenly. What was the case in the history of the first and last Adam must find its reflection in us. We have no ground of complaint that only in the future shall we possess the spiritual and heavenly body.

The principle indeed is stated in the most general terms, for we are not to supply σῶμα to τὸ πνευματικόν and to τὸ ψυχικόν.[1] We must take the neuters in the universality which they are so well fitted to express; and, thus taking them, the proposition is applicable, not to the human body alone, but to all things. Nor when we think of the perfection of the Deity, can we believe in the existence of any other principle. God could not be what we must suppose Him to be, were the law of an opposite kind, were the progression from a higher to a lower. Absolute perfection must desire to draw all things nearer to itself. Nay, may we not even go further, and say, that it is difficult to imagine the Almighty placing man upon the earth in his highest perfection at the very first? The most essential element of human perfection, the free choice and appropriation of the successive steps that lead to it, would then have been wanting. There could have been no moral training of the race. The precious fruits of discipline would have been unknown. We need not therefore ask, Why not perfection?—why not the spirit-life?—why not the spiritual body—now?

With what calmness does the thought of the Apostle teach us to contemplate the otherwise strange problem of human history! So far from complaining that we are not at once introduced to the perfection of our being, we learn to feel that the

[1] Comp. Moulton's *Winer*, p. 741; Ellicott *in loc*. Hofmann supplies σῶμα *in loc*.

first lowly estate of man was the pre-requisite of his moral growth. The fact that man was first formed only a living soul, so far from being full of nothing but perplexity, becomes, to one who recognises infinite love as the spring of all creation, the root out of which there grows the goodly tree of hope. That moral growth, that hope which impels to it,

> —— is man's distinctive mark alone,
> Not God's, and not the beast's. God is, they are,
> Man partly is, and wholly hopes to be.

"By hope were we saved: but hope that is seen is not hope: for who hopeth for that which he seeth? But if we hope for that which we see not, *then* do we with patience wait for it" (Rom. viii. 24, 25).

One other remark ought to be made. We are not to imagine that, while St. Paul has thus the idea of progress in his mind, he means by that progress continuous evolution, as if gradually, and by an infinite succession of small changes, the material passed into the sensuous, and the sensuous into the spiritual. Evolution has tried to bridge the chasm between matter and mind, but has failed to do so. St. Paul does not attempt to bridge it. Perhaps it never occurred to him that a bridge was necessary. He deals with a state of things, the existing conditions of which were acknowledged both by himself and others. Although, therefore, that state of things embodies a law of progress, it does not follow that the steps of the progress are to rise out of and above one another by a development which never ceases to operate. The great stages of the progress are rather marked by new creative acts. At the transition from the body of dust to ψυχή God interposes. At that from ψυχή to πνεῦμα He interposes again.

For the present we must pause. Let us, in doing so, recall for a moment what has been established. We have found the difficulties connected with the thought of the resurrection of the dead frankly and fully met. We have seen the course of human life on earth as it terminates in the grave set over against another course animated by a Divine spirit with the thought of which death is incompatible, and which is seen to be holding on in its eternal course in the person of the risen and glorified Lord. We have had set before us the principle from which we infer that, given the spirit-life of which experience tells, the spiritual body must be also given as its framework. And, finally, we have been taught to behold in all this, not something standing isolated from ordinary human history, but something graven in the deepest lines upon that history, in its first and in its last Adam, in its whole progress therefore from its earliest, and for our purpose at least lowest, to its highest stage. What we desire still further to know is, why we should be so closely connected with that history that it should repeat itself in us. If it can be shown us that it is reasonable that we should be, even if it be simply the fact that we are, thus closely connected with it, we can ask no more. We shall acquiesce in the Almighty's plan; and, believing that there will be a resurrection of the dead in the Lord who has already risen, we shall be ready to listen to the Apostle as he describes the particulars of an event so glorious, so far beyond all natural expectation or hope of man.

"*The first man is of the earth, earthy: the second man is of heaven. As is the earthy, such are they also that are earthy: and as is the heavenly, such are they also that are heavenly. And as we have borne the image of the earthy, we shall also bear the image of the heavenly.*"—1 COR. XV. 47-49. [R.V.]

Chapter x.

THE great law of progress, the great and glorious Divine plan, has been laid down and exhibited in the history of the first and last Adam, when compared with one another. "Howbeit that is not first which is spiritual, but that which is sensuous; then that which is spiritual." It remains only to be shown that our relation to these two Adams is such as to render it both reasonable and necessary that in their history ours should be repeated. To this the Apostle proceeds at ver. 47 of the chapter, first introducing the two Adams to us in a slightly different light from that in which he had presented them before, but at the same time in a light still more appropriate to his purpose. Then, having stated afresh, with this modification, the particular principle he has in view, he finally founds upon it a practical application.

I. *The two Adams.*—"The first man is of the earth, earthy: the Second Man is of heaven." It will be observed that the reading here adopted is different from that of the Authorized Version and the Textus Receptus, that text inserting ὁ Κύριος before the last words of the verse, ἐξ οὐρανοῦ. The necessity for the change of reading which consists in the omission of these words is so universally admitted, that, nothing further need be said except this, that demanded by external, the change is hardly less imperatively demanded by internal evidence. The aim of the two clauses is obviously to point out the *sources* out of which springs each of the two original "men" referred to; and that, for the purpose of leading to the inference, that according to the nature of the source will be also the nature of the head, and along with the head of the members of the body. The insertion of the Textus Receptus diverts our attention from this to a Divine personality of the Second Head, and destroys the directness of the contrast.

To what point of time then, we have again to ask, does St. Paul refer in each of the two clauses of this verse? "The first man is of the earth, earthy." The preposition "of" (ἐκ) unquestionably denotes origin, and we are thus taken to the time when Adam was formed out of "the dust of the ground" (Gen. ii. 7); that is, as before, to his original constitution, to a date anterior to the fall. Upon that point we need say no more. It is different with the second clause, "The Second Man is of heaven;" for, although it is allowed that the preposition (ἐκ) again denotes origin, no fewer than four different answers are here given to the question.

First, the reference is supposed to be to our

Lord's pre-incarnate state. So Baur, Beyschlag, and Pfleiderer. "Here however," says the last named scholar, "we cannot avoid thinking of the origin of the person of Christ from a heavenly pre-existence; for, as ἐξ οὐρανοῦ in this verse is given as the *ground* of the Second Adam having become spirit, so it cannot refer to that condition of the exalted One of which the Resurrection was the ground, but must refer to a heavenly condition which *preceded* the Resurrection, and consequently His whole earthly life, therefore to the condition of the heavenly *pre-existence*. Christ was enabled by His Resurrection to become the Second Adam, and the originator of a spiritual humanity, because He had always in Himself been so, because He did not owe His origin to merely natural humanity, but brought from heaven and put into it the quickening spiritual principle which had hitherto been wanting to it; in short, because He was essentially and originally (and not only from the time of His Resurrection) a heavenly man."[1] The immediate consequence of this view is to compel us to adopt the idea that "this human Person who had His origin *from* heaven, had also pre-existed in heaven *as man*, that is to say, as *spiritual man*, as the *same subject*, and in the *same form of existence* as that in which He continues to live in heaven as the exalted One."[2] The whole statement is founded upon the false notion that ἐξ

[1] *Paulinism*, translated by Peters, vol. i. p. 132.
[2] *Paulinism*, u.s. p. 139.

οὐρανοῦ necessarily points to the *ground* upon which our Lord was enabled to become "spirit." But the thought of such a *ground* of change is foreign to the text. St. Paul is occupied with the change which took place as *a fact*, not with the ground of it; besides which, when he says, in ver. 45, that "the last Adam became a life-giving spirit," he is certainly thinking of Him, not as spirit only, but as possessed of that spiritual body in which His spirit was housed, and without which He could, no more than any of His descendants, have been a living man, and so an "Adam." If however the spiritual body is thus to be transferred to our Lord's pre-incarnate state, the principle laid down in ver. 46 must be reversed, and the spiritual must precede the sensuous.

Secondly, it has been thought that the reference is to the Incarnation, because "Christ's heavenly origin is introduced in order to show the supernatural and Divine character of the renewed humanity which begins in Him."[1] But the Resurrection, the Ascension, and the heavenly life which followed them were themselves sufficient to show that our Lord was "of heaven," not of earth. Besides which, it may be asked, When did Christ's gift or power of renewing humanity begin? Was it at the Incarnation? or does it not rather appear from the whole course of the argument that the Apostle traces it to the time when Christ became "spirit" by His Resurrection? No doubt, even during His life on earth, He possessed

[1] Edwards *in loc.*

in Himself a renewed humanity, having a supernatural and Divine character. But did He then possess that humanity in such a way that He could be spoken of at that early stage as the spiritual Head of the renewed line of human beings to become what they were to be by descent from Him? Had He not then rather 'emptied Himself'? (Phil. ii. 7.) Had not He who was rich then for our sakes become poor? (2 Cor. viii. 9.) Was He not then limited and restrained by the arrangements of the Divine economy of salvation? And was it not at His Resurrection only that He entered upon that condition of existence in which He could be the head of the great family that was to spring from Him, and to be conformed to what He was? Besides this, it is to be observed that, in ver. 49, we are distinctly told that the image which we are to bear, and to which we are to press forward, is that of "the heavenly;" and the expression, which cannot be separated from the words "of heaven" in ver. 47, leads directly to the thought, not of the incarnate, but of the risen and glorified Lord to whom we are to be made like. It is not therefore with the thought of the Incarnate Lord, or, in other words, with the thought of the Incarnation, that the Apostle is occupied. The view of Principal Edwards appears, like that of Pfleiderer, to rest upon the impression that, in the words ἐξ οὐρανοῦ, we have a *ground* existing long previous to the specific point of time in the Apostle's mind, by the remembrance of which he would account for the fact that, at a later period, Christ became the first-born of God's spiritual children. Such a supposition is not called for. The course of argument hardly admits it. Man is all along regarded by St. Paul as one who when redeemed is not to be redeemed in spirit only, but to be clothed with a spiritual and heavenly body; and man obtains this because descended from One who, in His character as the Second Man, possesses such a body. It is not necessary therefore to go further back than the moment when our Lord obtained this spiritual body. Nay, if we do go further back, we must either think of the years during which our Lord possessed a limited body, and this will not suit the argument; or we must go further back still, to Christ's preexistent state. Edwards, who would object to the former, justly declines to do the latter, urging that it would be "fatal to the cogency of the argument, which depends on Christ's being Head of the race." Let it be observed however that, in whatever sense it may be true that Christ is "the Head of the race," it is not as the Head of "the race" that He is here spoken of. He is only the Head of His own line of spiritual descendants, in contrast with the race. Let it be further observed, that this line has the pledge and promise of a spiritual body only through the spirit-force bestowed upon it when Christ was glorified (John vii. 39), and it will be impossible for us to find the point $ἐξ\ οὐρανοῦ$ in the Incarnation.

Thirdly, it has been supposed that the reference

is to Christ's Second Coming. So Beet;[1] nor would it seem that such an idea is wholly wrong, for there can be little doubt that the Second Coming of his Lord, thought of by St. Paul as very near, was to him the season at which all that was most glorious for the believer culminated. But it is not in harmony with his teaching to say that Christ becomes the spiritual or heavenly man only at His Second Coming, or that only then does a spiritual or heavenly seed spring from Him. That seed springs from Him now. Throughout all the ages of the Church's history in the world He sends His Spirit into the hearts of His people, and in the possession of that Spirit they are His. It is true that not until the Second Coming do they actually receive the spiritual body; but from the instant when they are made one with Christ, they have the Spirit which includes that gift. They have the earnest, though not the completion, of their future state. In the renewed Spirit dwelling in their present body they have their victory over the flesh begun; and "if the Spirit of Him that raised up Jesus from the dead dwelleth in you, He that raised up Christ Jesus from the dead shall quicken also your mortal bodies through His Spirit that dwelleth in you" (Rom. viii. 11).

Fourthly, there remains only the Resurrection of our Lord for the time of ἐξ οὐρανοῦ, although with this ought to be taken the thoughts of the Ascension and Glorification, which can never be separated from it.

[1] Comp. Hofmann, *Schriftbeweis*, vol. i. p. 148 ; Godet *in loc.*

Then our Lord broke the bonds of earth. Then He assumed the unlimited for the limited, the spiritual for the material, the eternal for the temporal. Then He was fully ἐξ οὐρανοῦ. Then, as the writer of the Epistle to the Hebrews says, "Christ having come a high priest of the good things to come, through the greater and more perfect tabernacle, not made with hands, that is to say, not of this creation, nor yet through the blood of goats and calves, but through His own blood, entered in once for all into the holy place, having obtained eternal redemption" (Heb. ix. 11, 12). The words "of heaven" therefore point us to the super-earthly, the heavenly source out of which at His Resurrection, Ascension, and Glorification came the super-earthly, the heavenly, life of Christ. It is the life upon which He then entered that is transmitted, both in spirit and in body, to such as are descended from Him.

Another change in St. Paul's mode of expression in this verse deserves notice. The two stages of man's progress are no longer spoken of exactly as in the previous verses. They are no longer the "sensuous" and the "spiritual": they are the "earthy" and the "heavenly." The change is easily accounted for. What perplexed the Corinthian sceptics was the thought that it was impossible for the dead to rise in the body in which they died; and that, even were they to do so, such a body would be altogether unsuitable to the "heavenly" abode of the risen Lord. They had discussed among themselves, not the "sensuous" and the "spiritual," but the "earthy" and the "heavenly." This leads to the mention of the latter rather than the former pair. The first man, it was at once to be admitted, was not merely "sensuous," he was "earthy." He was made of the dust or soil of earth; for it is said that "the Lord God formed man of the dust of the ground" (Gen. ii. 7). To earth therefore he would naturally return. But over against this had to be set the fact that the Second Man was "of heaven," the very heaven promised to the saints, out of that heaven, in the particular origin which is thought of here, just as the other was in his origin out "of earth." If therefore the doubters allowed that the first man connected them with earth, they must equally allow that the Second Man, if they sprang from Him, must connect them with heaven. Thus the Apostle is led to a fuller statement of this truth.

II. *The principle making it appear both reasonable and necessary that the history of the two Adams should repeat itself in that of believers.*—The principle is stated in the words of ver. 48: "As is the earthy, such are they also that are earthy: and as is the heavenly, such are they also that are heavenly." It rests upon that similarity between a progenitor and his descendants, the thought of which has been all along in the mind of the Apostle, and which only needed the fuller statement that it now receives. That there was, that there must be, such a similarity, no one to whom this epistle was written would deny. It had been one of the commonplaces of Jewish, it was one of the commonplaces of Christian, thought. It is a principle, not only of man's religious, but of his ordinary history. It is borne witness to by all experience. Nor does it keep the world stagnant. It throws no obstacle in the way of that progress which we have seen to be one of the great laws of God. It is rather a chief foundation of improvement, a constant stimulus to us to improve. By strict attention to God's requirements we can make ourselves better, stronger, fairer, happier than we are at any particular moment of our history. Can there be a more animating thought than that, according to the Divine plan, these blessings will not be confined to us, but will also be transmitted to our children? There is of course always the possibility that our children may despise and reject them, for they are moral beings as well as we; but, under the operation of this law, they may enter upon the struggle of life with possibilities of good which might not otherwise have been theirs; and, as man is constituted, few considerations are fitted to exercise over him a more beneficial influence than this, that he benefits others dear to him when he benefits himself.

The law then to which St. Paul alludes and its beneficial influence are equally unquestionable. But the chief point to be attended to at present in connexion with it is, that the Apostle must be understood to refer to it in its widest sense. He is thinking of it as applicable, not merely to the body, but to the spirit of man. "The headship of Adam involves identity of nature and of character with those who are his; the headship of Christ involves identity of nature and of character with those who are in union with Him. Because Adam was ψυχικός and χοϊκός, all men in their natural state are terrestrial; because Christ is ἐπουράνιος and πνευματικός, all believers are in their supernatural state spiritual and heavenly. The indefinite word τοιοῦτος is 'purposely chosen.'"[1] To give this full meaning to the Apostle's words is necessary in order to do justice to the argument. Yet we are not to suppose that he is dealing with man as fallen under the dominion of sin. We have seen already that this was not the case at ver. 45, and, again, that it was not the case at ver. 47. It is not more the case now than it was on either of these occasions. The identity or the similarity between the head and the descendants extends no further than the thought of their sensuous condition on the one hand, or their condition as ruled by a spirit life-force on the other; and, though this latter force, being that of the Spirit of Christ, is necessarily holy, the holiness is not prominently in view. St. Paul, in short, has still his eye upon men as descended from "sensuous" not fallen Adam, and upon Christ as "spirit," without dwelling upon the ethical characteristics of that word.

[1] Edwards, *in loc.*

A difficulty may be started here which it may be well to notice for a moment. There is a want of similarity, it may be said, between the two descents upon which St. Paul is reasoning. That from the Second Adam is immediate; that from the first is mediated through many generations. We stand in direct and personal connexion with the Second Man, from whom, as a living Lord, we each moment receive the Spirit. We stand in connexion with the first man as part of a race rather than as individuals. The answer to the difficulty is twofold. (1) The first Adam lives on in all his descendants; and so long therefore as we are in that line of descent we may be said to be immediately connected with him. The lengthened period between him and us disappears from view. As much as Cain and Abel may we say of ourselves, We are the children of Adam. His earthy nature is as truly ours as it was theirs. (2) If it is as part of a race that we are in the first man, as part also of a community or race we are in the Second Man. Through the Church as a Divine institution in the world, through her life and organization, through her sacraments and worship, the blessings of Christ's kingdom flow to the individual member of the kingdom. Christ lives in His Church; and, when we are really in His Church, we are in Him. By His living, personal presence the Church is made at every moment what she is,—His Body. The body is not less real in the one case than in the other; and each believer is not less truly a member of the body, and grows up to what he is by being so, than each man is a member of the race, with all the consequences depending on that fact. No essential difference therefore is produced by this, that the head of the sensuous line of descendants returned long since to the dust, while the Head of the spiritual line of descendants is living now.

III.—*The Apostle has closed his argument and it remains for him only to follow it up with a practical exhortation suited to the circumstances.* The exhortation is contained in the words of ver. 49 : " And as we have borne the image of the earthy, let us also bear the image of the heavenly." An important word of the verse is no doubt the subject of dispute. Shall we read φορέσομεν or φορέσωμεν, " we shall bear " or " let us bear " ? The former is the reading of the Textus Receptus, and is adopted alike in the Authorized and Revised Versions, although the Revised informs us in the margin that " many ancient authorities read, let us bear." In point of fact the case might have been put more strongly, no ancient MS. except B supporting the indicative form, while versions, Fathers, and even the bulk of modern MSS. follow the preponderating mass of the ancients. To adopt in such circumstances the reading " we shall bear " would be little else than to construct the text of Scripture according to our own fancy, and not according to the evidence. " Let us bear " is accordingly read by all the best modern editors ; and, even although the meaning were more obscure than it is, it might be our duty to accept it, trusting, as has happened in so many other instances of a similar kind, that we should yet see more clearly.

In reality however the meaning, so far from being obscure, is in a high degree interesting and forcible. It depends upon the signification to be attached to the word εἰκών or "image." That word can hardly be applied to the resemblance which the spiritual *bodies* of the redeemed, viewed apart from their spirits, shall hereafter possess to the spiritual *body* of the Risen Lord. It appears to express complete resemblance to, and, combined with this, derivation from, that of which it is the image.[1] Thus Christ is the εἰκών of God, in whom the illuminating power of the Divine glory shines so as to illuminate others (2 Cor. iv. 4); at once the representation and the manifestation of Him who is invisible (Col. i. 15; comp. Lightfoot *in loc.*). Thus in this very epistle Christians, beheld in Christ their Head (chap. xi. 3), are also the εἰκών of God (chap. xi. 7), for they have put off the old man and put on the new man, which is being renewed unto a perfect knowledge "after the image of Him that created" them (Col. iii. 10); and they have at the same time been "transformed into the image" of the glorified Lord who is "Spirit" (2 Cor. iii. 18). Thus also the writer of the Epistle to the Hebrews tells us that the law proved its imperfection by the fact that it was no more than "a shadow" of the good things to come, not the very εἰκών of the things; it could not set forth these future good things in all their reality

[1] Trench, *Synonyms of the New Testament*, § xv. p. 58.

and fulness (Heb. x. 1). And, once more, it is thus that in the Apocalypse the second beast is spoken of as inducing men to make an εἰκών of the first beast, so that "the image of the beast should both speak, and cause that as many as should not worship the image of the beast should be killed" (Rev. xiii. 15). This "image of the beast" is obviously his representative, his manifestation among men, the embodiment of his cruel worldly power.

In the light of such usage the meaning of the word εἰκών in the verse before us ought to be sufficiently clear. It cannot be confined to the thought of bodily likeness alone to the glorified body of the Risen Lord. Even at an earlier point of the chapter we have found that a limitation of this kind could not be justified, and that σῶμα is not to be supplied to the τὸ πνευματικόν and the τὸ ψυχικόν of ver. 46. Throughout the whole argument, too, the thought of the resemblance of the believer both in spirit and in body to his Lord has been, if not prominently brought forward, yet in St. Paul's mind. The communication of the spirit of Christ, leading to conformity with the body of Christ, has been the implied foundation of all that he has said; and it can therefore occasion no surprise that, before he closes, he should look at the relation between the Head and the members in its widest sense.

The moment this is admitted the force and beauty of the reading φορέσωμεν, "let us bear," instead of "we shall bear," rises to view. Read the latter, and we have a comparatively tame repetition of what has been already said. Read the former, and, with minds filled and elevated by the ennobling prospect which has been set before us, we pass into the wide field of our own corresponding obligations. We are reminded that the whole matter is one in which moral action on our own part is implied. Not by mechanical force are we made partakers of the spirit and life of Christ, but by willing appropriation of what He bestows. We must act our part. We must freely receive what Christ freely gives. We must exhibit all diligence in making our calling and election sure. Therefore may St. Paul well say, " Let us bear the image of the heavenly." We have been too much the children of the first Adam alone. We have been bound by earthly ties, carried away by earthly affections, limited by earthly hopes. The sensuous side of our life is always pressed upon by the things of sense, by

> The beauty, and the wonder, and the power,
> The shapes of things, their colours, lights, and shades,
> Changes, surprises,—and God made it all !

We need to be reminded that, however important and valuable that side of our life may be, there is another side, deeper, truer, and more enduring in its character, heavenly not earthly, and with results for eternity as well as time. We have had, and still have, the one life ; we may have, and ought to have, the other. The heavenly Lord lives to communicate His Spirit to us, and He invites us to be one with

Him. "As" therefore "we have borne the image of the earthy, let us also bear the image of the heavenly." Then we may travel onwards on our journey, and fight our battle, whatever it may be, in the sure hope of a blessed resurrection to a heavenly Lord in a heavenly life.

" Now this I say, brethren, that flesh and blood cannot inherit the kingdom of God ; neither doth corruption inherit incorruption. Behold, I tell you a mystery : We shall not all sleep, but we shall all be changed, in a moment, in the twinkling of an eye, at the last trump : for the trumpet shall sound, and the dead shall be raised incorruptible, and we shall be changed."—1 COR. xv. 50-52. [R.V.]

Chapter xi.

AT the moment when the Apostle reaches the point before us, "the image of the heavenly," spoken of at the close of ver. 49, fills his mind and transports him with joy and triumph. "As we have borne the image of the earthy, let us also bear the image of the heavenly," had been his cry. Let us see that we be found among the number of those who belong to the line of spiritual descendants of which the Second Adam is the Head, so that we may experience a resurrection from the dead similar to His, and may receive the body of "incorruption," of "glory," and of "power," the "spiritual" and "heavenly" body. Suddenly he seems now to turn to the thought that the obtaining of this body had, throughout all his previous argument, been associated with, or even conditioned by, the preliminary experience of death. But all Christians were not destined to die. In the great day of the Lord's Second Coming there would be those living upon the earth whom he elsewhere describes as the "we that are alive, that are left unto the coming of the Lord" (1 Thess. iv. 15). They would be living in their ordinary bodies, in their bodies of "corruption," of "dishonour," and of "weakness," in their "sensuous" and "earthy" bodies, in bodies adapted to this material and fleeting world, and unfitted for that glorious kingdom of God which would then be manifested. What therefore was to become of them? Were they not to share in the blessedness of those who, being one with Christ, were "children of God; and if children, then heirs; heirs of God, and joint-heirs with Christ; if so be that we suffer with Him, that we may be also glorified with Him" (Rom. viii. 16, 17)? Curiously enough, the misapprehension is exactly the converse of that with which the Apostle had to deal in writing to the disciples at Thessalonica. There the fear was that they who had died before the Second Coming of the Lord would not partake of the blessedness prepared for such as would be alive when the Lord descends "with a shout, with the voice of the archangel, and with the trump of God;" and assurance had to be given that the dead in Christ shall "rise first." Here the difficulty sprang up in connexion with those who would be alive when Jesus came. The bright prospects hitherto spoken of in this chapter had been connected with a passage through the grave. What shall be the fate of those for whom the providence of God prepares no such passage?

Such seem to be the thoughts occupying the mind of St. Paul when he comes to the fiftieth verse of this chapter; and, if it be so, not only the general strain of the following verses is at once explained, but light is thrown upon individual expressions, the full meaning of which we might not otherwise perceive.

"But this I say, brethren, that flesh and blood cannot inherit the kingdom of God: neither doth corruption inherit incorruption." Τοῦτο δέ φημι, "But this I say," introducing an emphatic and positive assertion, not intended to explain more fully what has been said already, but to lead the way to a new consideration connected with it (comp. chap. vii. 29). That "flesh and blood" are here used to denote only the physical nature of man, without taking into account, under the word "flesh," the lusts and passions of our lower nature,[1] there can be no doubt; but it is of more consequence to observe that, if the view of the connexion above spoken of be correct, it is concrete men, men then alive, rather than the materials of which their bodies are composed, that the Apostle has in his eye. In that condition in which he is now dealing with them, they are "flesh and blood;" and, as such, they are also "corruption." The two expressions refer to the same thing, and there is no ground whatever for the supposition—a supposition rather breaking the continuity of the Apostle's statement—that "flesh and blood" denote those who shall be alive at the *Parousia*, and that "corruption" denotes those who shall have died before it.[2] The word "corruption" applies to the body, not only when in the grave, but in its present state of existence

[1] As Cox, p. 227.   [2] As Godet *in loc.*

upon earth (comp. ver. 42); and both clauses refer to living men, although, according to the common method of Scripture, the second is climactic to the first. The word "inherit" is here interesting, and has light shed on it when we fix our thoughts on the general purport of the verse. The covenant with Abraham hardly seems to be alluded to;[1] it is of the heirship of Romans viii. 17 that St. Paul is thinking, that heirship which is given us with Christ Himself, "the Heir" (comp. Matt. xxi. 38; Heb. i. 2), when we trace our spiritual descent from Him, when we are in Him, and are one with Him. The law, then, thus laid down by St. Paul is not only general and absolute, but founded in the very nature of things. In the same way as our Lord had said, "Except a man be born anew, he *cannot* see the kingdom of God" (John iii. 3), so the Apostle says, "Flesh and blood" *cannot* inherit that kingdom when it is revealed in glory. In the second clause, in which the word "cannot" is not employed, there is probably no less of a climax to the first clause than there was when the mention of "corruption" followed the mention of "flesh and blood." The present tense, "doth inherit," seems to do more than negative the thought of what might otherwise happen at any particular instant. It gives expression to the Divine, everlasting, and unchanging plan, and in this respect it may be said to be of even greater force than the "cannot" of the preceding clause.

[1] As Edwards.

"Flesh and blood" then, or "corruption," that is, the men and women who would be alive upon the earth when Christ was manifested, could not enter as they were into the kingdom. What was to be their fate? They would not be in the position of those who had passed through the seed-bed of the grave. Dead believers would be raised, ready for the kingdom. But these had not died. They were, by the supposition, in their earthly bodies; and earthly bodies are, alike by the nature of the case and the Divine plan, unfit for the kingdom. What then was to happen to them? Everything makes it plain, and the point ought to be fixed with the greatest possible distinctness in our minds, that St. Paul is thinking only of those who shall be alive at the *Parousia*, and that the mystery of which he is about to tell us has reference to them alone.

This mystery is now stated, vers. 51, 52, in the following words, taken from the Revised Version, which is here in the closest correspondence with the Authorized: "Behold, I tell you a mystery: We shall not all sleep, but we shall all be changed, in a moment, in the twinkling of an eye, at the last trump: for the trumpet shall sound, and the dead shall be raised incorruptible, and we shall be changed."

Before endeavouring to ascertain the meaning of these words, it is necessary to determine the best attested reading of the Greek; and this the more, that the various readings of ver. 51 open up principles of textual criticism as interesting and important as those of any single text in the New Testament. There are three such readings; but one of them (that which gives us ἀναστησόμεθα instead of κοιμηθησόμεθα) is of little consequence, and we may confine ourselves to the two that remain.

The first (A) is substantially that of the Textus Receptus, πάντες οὐ κοιμηθησόμεθα ; the second (B) assigns a different position to the negative particle, placing it, not before, but after κοιμηθησόμεθα, and before the second πάντες: πάντες κοιμηθησόμεθα οὐ πάντες δὲ ἀλλαγησόμεθα. The most remarkable circumstance connected with these two readings is, that while all the most valuable diplomatic evidence, with the exception of the *Codex Vaticanus*, is in favour of the second (B), critics generally, including even Westcott and Hort, whose adherence to this department of evidence is so steadfast, and has been attended with such momentous consequences to the New Testament text, have been constrained to decide, upon internal grounds, in favour of the first (A).[1] In short, we have here a case, one of very few of the kind, in which the ablest inquirers have felt themselves compelled to allow that external evidence must yield to internal. And why? Because, supposing (A) to be the correct reading, the genesis of (B) can be at once explained; because, supposing (B) to be correct, the genesis of (A) would be inexplicable. What we shall immediately see to be the true

[1] Comp. also Tregelles, Tischendorf, etc.

meaning of (A) must have appeared either so unintelligible or so startling to the Church, that she must have considered it out of the question to acquiesce in it. The reading, she would reason, must be false; and the second reading (B) would suggest itself as a simple method of meeting the difficulty, and of making the words of the Apostle worthy, as they must have been, of his Divine commission. The meaning of the first reading, the only meaning of which it is naturally susceptible, is, "All of us shall not-fall-asleep," or, in other words, "None of us shall fall-asleep." In the course of a few years therefore, to say nothing of generations, it could not but be seen that that statement was disproved by fact. The meaning of the second reading is, "All of us shall fall asleep, but not all of us (*i.e.* some of us) shall be changed;" or, to put it in another way, St. Paul says first, "All of us shall fall asleep," and then suddenly correcting himself, he adds, "Yet not all of us: some of us shall be changed." A satisfactory sense, or at least, a sense in conformity with fact, appeared thus to be gained. The future would be as the past until the end of the present dispensation. Falling asleep would continue as before; but the great day would come, and then some of those living at the time would be changed. These considerations suggest the probable history of the manner in which the second reading (B) found its way into so wide a circle of authorities. But the greater the degree of probability with which we can account, on subjective grounds, for the introduction of a contested reading into the text, the less is that reading entitled to claim its place as the original utterance of the writer. The weight of external evidence on behalf of (B) is thus considerably diminished.

Nor is even the sense afforded by it so good as to weigh much in its favour. If it relieves us from the peculiar difficulty attaching to (A), it has difficulties of its own to contend with not less serious. One of two meanings must be attached to it. (1) The "all" in the two clauses may be understood, in its widest sense, as applicable to men without exception; in which case the meaning is, All shall die, but only believers shall be changed. Thus introducing a reference to non-believers, this meaning may be set aside without any argument against it upon other grounds. There is no more striking characteristic of the whole chapter than the degree to which it ignores the existence of unbelievers. (2) The "all" may be understood in a more limited sense as applying only to believers; and, as already indicated, the Apostle may be understood to say, "All of us shall die; yet not all of us: some of us shall be changed." But, apart from the awkwardness of the limitation "all, yet not all," what could lead the Apostle to give prominence to the fact that those of whom he is thinking shall fall asleep or die? He has passed away from that state of things. He has nothing to do now with either death or resurrection from the grave. He has turned to a different class of persons, in whose case there was neither death nor resurrection. He could hardly therefore have spoken in the manner supposed. On every ground the second reading must be rejected, and the first reading, that of the Textus Receptus, must stand. The Apostle says, πάντες οὐ κοιμηθησόμεθα, πάντες δὲ ἀλλαγησόμεθα. What is his meaning? And, if his meaning be that naturally suggested by the words, is there any legitimate method of escape from the charge that it has been disproved by fact?

It would be vain to attempt to enter into all the speculations of grammarians and commentators as to the correct mode of rendering negative sentences cast in the mould of that before us, or to discuss at length the different interpretations which have been given to the Apostle's words: "All of us shall not sleep," *i.e.* none of us shall sleep; "All of us shall not sleep," *i.e.* some of us shall sleep; "All of us shall not sleep," *i.e.* some of us shall be awake or alive. It is enough to say that the general contention is, that in biblical Greek the position of the negatives is not so rigorously observed as in the classic style; and that, although therefore the οὐ is, strictly speaking, to be connected with the verb, its sense may be trajected to the subject "all." We thus obtain the meaning which may be given in the words of Godet (*in loc*): "We shall not all die—there will be living Christians when the Lord comes again; but we shall all require to be changed—living believers by transformation, the dead by resurrection." This view cannot be accepted. It is no doubt urged that we may overcome the grammatical difficulty of trajecting the οὐ from the verb to its subject πάντες by a comparison of such a passage as that always quoted in defence of this procedure, Numbers xxiii. 13, in which Balak says to Balaam μέρος τι αὐτοῦō ψει, πάντας δὲ οὐ μὴ ἴδῃς, and where, to keep the negative in close connexion with the verb, would make Balak contradict himself : " a part shalt thou see, but all shalt thou not-see," *i.e.* " none shalt thou see." Or we are referred to such words as those of Romans iii. 20, οὐ δικαιωθήσεται πᾶσα σάρξ, where the tendency of the Hebrew mind to connect with the verb the negative belonging to the subject is thought to be illustrated. This solution of the difficulty, however, is extremely doubtful. Its possibility is indeed denied in the strongest terms by, amongst others, Winer and Meyer.[1] But even though it

[1] A moment's consideration indeed may show us that Numb. xxiii. 13 is no proper parallel to the present passage. There can be there no mistake as to the meaning, the first part of the sentence stating distinctly that Balaam shall see only a part of the host. With this the second part of the sentence must agree. Nor does it make any difference in the thought of that second part whether we connect the negative with the πάντας or the ἴδῃς: "not all shalt thou see," or "all (the emphasis lying on this word) shalt thou not see." That the second passage, Rom. iii. 20, is equally useless for the purpose for which it is referred to appears from this, that if we traject the negative, connecting it with the subject of the verb, instead of the verb itself, we obtain a sense utterly at variance with the statement which the Apostle is concerned to prove : "Wherefore by the works of the law shall be justified not all flesh," or "not all flesh shall be justified," *i.e.* "some flesh shall be justified." It would seem, therefore, as if both these passages were improperly appealed to for the object they are supposed to serve.

were grammatically possible, it is rendered wholly inadmissible on account of the double meaning which it puts into ἀλλαγησόμεθα—that of a change in some by transformation, in others by resurrection. Nothing can well be more certain than that, throughout the passage (comp. especially ver. 53, where the two acts are clearly distinguished), that verb is used in one sense alone, the sense of change by *transformation*. In these circumstances there seems to be no alternative but to abide by the simple and natural meaning of the words, and to understand the Apostle as saying, "We all (*i.e.* all included in the πάντες) shall not fall asleep, but we all (*i.e.* all again included in the πάντες) shall be changed."

The propriety of so rendering is confirmed by one or two different considerations that may be noticed before speaking of the difficulty to which the rendering gives rise. (*a*) It preserves the connexion between the negative and the verb, as in 1 John ii. 19, "They went out, that they might be made manifest how that they all are not of us," where it is not so much the object of the Apostle to say that there are false members of the Christian community, as to say that none of those who, by going out, prove themselves to be so, ever really belonged to it. Although the order of the words in St. John is slightly different (yet only as regards emphasis) from that of the words before us, the negative is thus to be closely connected with its verb. So also 1 John ii. 21, "Every lie is-not (οὐκ ἔστι) of the truth;" *i.e.* it is the essence of every lie that it does not spring from the truth. (*b*) The rendering now defended strictly preserves the same meaning for πάντες in both clauses. The persons of whom it is asserted that they shall not die are the very same persons of whom it is said that they shall be changed. We all, whoever we are, shall not die, but we shall all be changed. (*c*) It preserves what would appear to be almost the technical meaning of ἀλλαγησόμεθα in vers. 51 and 52 ; for, as has been already stated, that word is so used as to make it impossible to include under it the " change " which is to take effect upon those who have been asleep or dead. Besides which, the idea of " change " will not suit the condition of the dead. Change supposes something to be changed, a person on whom the change is to operate. But the dead are buried out of sight. They have returned to corruption. They are not there to be changed. What they need is to be raised up in another form ; and that resurrection they shall experience. This " change," whatever may be said to the contrary, cannot include resurrection. It refers only to transmutation. (*d*) Thus preserving the special meaning of the word " changed," we preserve also the distinction clearly drawn in ver. 52 between the νεκροί (the dead) and the ἡμεῖς (we). (*e*) We have a meaning of precisely that kind which would be likely to startle the Church, and to lead it insensibly to modify the Greek. (*f*) On the other supposition the whole difficulty, to be immediately referred to, is not removed. From the ἡμεῖς of ver. 52 St. Paul cannot exclude himself. The meaning of the words can hardly be any other than this, that none of the "we all" shall die, that all of the "we all" shall be changed.

It is not to be denied that we are thus face to face with a very serious difficulty. We seem to be forced by the principles of fair exegesis to make St. Paul say in a distinct and positive manner what has been contradicted by fact; and we make him say this too at a time when to any observer his statement must have appeared to be at variance with what was actually passing around him. Can the Apostle really intend to convey to us the assurance that the last Christian of that generation who was to pass through the gate of the grave had already died? Was no other to follow into the valley of the shadow of death? And can he say this at a moment when, in all probability, many Christians at Corinth were "weak and sickly, and not a few sleep" (κοιμῶνται, 1 Cor. xi. 30)? Is it so that, according to the statement of the Apostle, there was to be no more death, and that all believers had only to wait for a more or less immediate "change"? To say the least of it, this is exceedingly unlike St. Paul; and not only so, it is out of keeping with that mind of Christ which we know to have been his authority, and which he so often shows us he had made his own. Let the following observations be considered:

1. It does not seem difficult to account for the peculiar form of the expression, for the negative

instead of the positive form, "we shall not-sleep." Throughout his whole previous argument the Apostle had dealt with *sleeping* or dying as the main point of the great transition he had in view. The perplexity in the minds of his readers did not present itself in the form, "What if we shall not be alive?" so much as in the form, "What if we shall not have died?" Hence he is led to designate those of whom he is thinking, not as persons who shall be alive, but as persons who shall not-have-died.

2. But what of the πάντες (all)? What of a statement so universal, and apparently applied without any limitation to himself and the men around him? The explanation is to be found in St. Paul's habit of thought and in the mode in which, under the influence of that habit, he is led to express himself. When a thought takes possession of his mind, it wholly fills it. He can look at it only in one light, and apart from the qualifications and limitations with which, in cooler and less eager minds, it would naturally be associated. What he dwells upon starts up before him like a picture, the canvas of which is entirely occupied with one conception. The picture is his own. He is in the midst of it. He is one with the figures filling it. For the time he is incapable of admitting any thought by which the leading idea of the picture would require to be balanced, if we are to have all the truth. Illustrations of this habit in its more general form are so numerous and so commonly admitted, that it is unnecessary to speak of them.

It is more to our present purpose to refer to one in this very chapter, in which the same word πάντες is treated exactly as it is here. At ver. 22 we read, "For as in Adam all die, so also in Christ shall all be made alive." No statement could be more general, and both the use made of it and the conclusions deduced from it in that form are well known. Yet nothing can be more certain than that "all" here is not "all" in its universal aspect. Those intended are only "all" to the Apostle. Whence comes this? His mind was filled in the verses coming immediately before with the thought of those who wake from their sleep to be presented along with Christ, the first-fruits, to the Father, with the thought of those who share with the Risen Saviour the resurrection of the dead. He had been gazing on them as they passed before him, a glorious army, clothed in all the splendour which he afterwards endeavours to describe by speaking of "this corruptible putting on incorruption, and this mortal putting on immortality" (ver. 53). The canvas is full; not another figure can find a place in it; these sons of the resurrection morning are all upon whom he can fix his thoughts, and he cries out, though having reference to them alone, "For as in Adam all die, so also in Christ shall all be made alive."

It is precisely the same thing here. At ver. 50, as we have already seen, St. Paul had been speaking of concrete living Christians as contrasted with Christians who had died. The latter were a complete class; so then also are the former. They come before the Apostle in all their perplexity, as for the moment they think, not only that they may not, but that they will not die. Is there no hope for them? St. Paul identifies himself with them. He is in the midst of a new company, and the company of such as had died is forgotten. He is one with the new company, and he makes the new company one with him. We are to live, he exclaims; by the supposition we are not to die. "We all" belong to those who are not to fall asleep. What then? We belong to those who in that case will be changed; and our hope is as sure and precious as that of others. This power of identifying himself with others is a true trait of the great Apostle. "Who," he exclaims, writing on one occasion to the Corinthian Church, "is weak, and I am not weak? Who is made to stumble, and I burn not?" (2 Cor. xi. 29); and in this very epistle, "To the Jews I became as a Jew, that I might gain Jews; to them that are under the law, as under the law, that I might gain them that are under the law; to them that are without law, as without law, that I might gain them that are without law; to the weak I became weak, that I might gain the weak: I am become all things to all men, that I may by all means save some" (1 Cor. ix. 20-22). It is by no means necessary, therefore, to think that the Apostle lays it down as a fact, that none of the men of that generation would die. It might have been so. It might be so with the men of this generation. None of us knows the hour when the Lord cometh, and no one knows that better of his own day than St. Paul knew it of his day. Enough that he is dealing with one half only of a great truth. The first half had been disposed of. Christians who die shall rise to a more glorious life. The second half comes next. Christians who do not die shall be fitted for the Divine glory by being changed.

Let us paraphrase the Apostle's words: "I have been dealing with the thought of death as of that crisis in the believer's history through which he passes from the corruption, the dishonour, and the weakness of earth to the incorruption, the glory, and the power of the future and heavenly life; and I have spoken as I have done because the difficulties proposed to me had reference to the condition of the departed. 'How are the dead raised up? and with what manner of body do they come?' Do not imagine, however, that I am insensible to the fact that the Second Coming of the Lord of which I have so often spoken in my teaching will find many of His people alive upon the earth. They, it is true, shall not die. They shall not pass through that grave which is the ultimate form of the seed-bed out of which, like grains of wheat springing up into the plant, Christians who have died shall spring up into their future glorious estate. Those who have died shall not on that account anticipate them. They shall be changed." And then he passes on, with a full mind unburdening itself, to some of the particulars of the change.

It will take place "in a moment, in the twinkling of an eye." There is no need to dwell upon the figure employed in the second of these clauses, which is obviously intended to bring out, like the "moment" spoken of, the suddenness of the change. There is no gradual development, no process of refining or spiritualizing of the body that may have been going on for years or centuries. Whatever may have happened in that way in no degree interferes with the instantaneousness of the final issue. This instantaneousness may indeed startle us, but there is also much that may help us to appreciate, if not fully to comprehend it. The first step taken in any new and great series of events must be always sudden. It may have been long prepared for, as the gathering forces of electricity in the atmosphere prepare for the moment when the equilibrium shall be restored; but, when that is restored, it is with the suddenness of the lightning's flash. Creation, in whatever form we think of it, whether as innumerable atoms in ill-assorted whirl, or as a well-ordered and harmonious system, must have been sudden. The transition from not-being to being could be nothing else. Astronomers too are familiar with great cataclysms in the history of the universe around them. They behold stars suddenly broken up, lights with which they have been long familiar disappear, and new lights come into existence. With what tremendous changes all this must have been accompanied, they cannot tell; but this they know that, whatever their extent, they must have been sudden. So also now. It may help us the better to comprehend the teaching of this passage if we bear in mind that the change referred to does not take place while the ordinary processes of nature are going on with their usual regularity and calmness. Nature prepares us for convulsions. Scripture tells us that it is in the midst of one of these that what is here spoken of will take place. It is the day of the Lord, and "the day of the Lord will come as a thief; in the which the heavens shall pass away with a great noise, and the elements shall be dissolved with fervent heat, and the earth and the works that are therein shall be burned up" (2 Pet. iii. 10). Who shall estimate aright the changes on every side, and on every object with which earth is filled, that may and must accompany this great change? To imagine men passing through it unchanged would be the difficulty, and whatever change takes place will certainly be "in a moment, in the twinkling of an eye."

Another mark of the great era in human history spoken of is added by the Apostle—"at the last trump." The trumpet is the same as that of which we read in the First Epistle to the Thessalonians, when it is there said that "the Lord Himself shall descend from heaven, with a shout, with the voice of the archangel, and with the trump of God" (chap. iv. 16). Still more particularly, it is that of which our Lord Himself spoke to His disciples in His discourse upon the last things : " And He shall send forth His angels with the great sound of a trumpet, and they shall gather together His elect from the four winds, from one end of heaven to the other" (Matt. xxiv. 31). This gathering together of Christ's elect is now before the Apostle's eye; and the sounding of the trumpet long and loud,—so long that the sound travels to every region of the earth, so loud that it penetrates the deepest chambers of the tomb—is to him the symbol of the gathering.

The greatness of the occasion, too, is increased by the circumstance that this trumpet shall then sound for the "last" time. It had sounded at the giving of the law, so that, even amidst the thunders that re-echoed amongst the mountains of Horeb, it was heard "exceeding loud" (Exod. xix. 16). From the thought of it, as the suitable accompaniment of all great occasions when the Almighty manifested Himself to Israel, came no doubt its employment in connexion with the fall of Jericho, with the peculiar solemnities of the seventh month, the greatest month in Israel's sacred year, and with those solemn assemblies of the people of which it was said, " Blow the trumpet in Zion, call a solemn assembly" (Joel ii. 15). All along the history of Israel it had been associated with the most momentous events which befell that people. But this sounding shall be the "last." The trumpet will be no more needed to accompany the giving of a law, for the law has been written upon the Christian heart; no more needed to summon the

Israel of God to the overthrow of hostile powers, for all Israel's enemies have been overcome; no more needed to introduce great festivals which are to last for a few days, for the Feast of Tabernacles has begun which is to endure for ever; and no more needed to call solemn assemblies soon to be broken up, for the solemn assembly now convened is never to be dissolved. Therefore this trumpet is the "last."

The heart of St. Paul appears to swell with peculiar emotion when he thinks of this feature of the great day of which he speaks, for he comes back upon it, without repeating anything that he had said of the other characteristics of the day. "For," he adds, "the trumpet shall sound."

Then follows the effect, "And the dead shall be raised incorruptible, and we shall be changed." The two classes of which he had been speaking are still before him,—the dead, and they who are alive at the Lord's coming. Of the one he says that they shall be raised, and that no longer in the state of corruption; *i.e.* of weakness and decay and liability to death in which they had lived on earth, but incorruptible. Of the other he says simply, without as yet specifying the characteristics of the change, "and we shall be changed." Many attempts, more or less plausible, have been made to show that under the "we" thus spoken of the Apostle does not necessarily include himself, and that he thus leaves no imputation to be made upon the accuracy of that view of the future which it is thought his inspiration must have secured to him. These attempts can hardly be said to have been successful; and all that it seems possible to contend for is, that there is no dogmatic assertion of the fact that he and the men of that generation would certainly be alive when the Lord came. As, at ver. 51, he can hardly be understood to maintain that no one of his own generation, including himself, will die before that time, so he can hardly be understood to maintain here that he and they will certainly be then alive. He may have thought it highly probable that such would be the case; and the tone of his earlier writings, as in the two Epistles to the Thessalonians (for the Second Epistle to the Thessalonians teaches upon this point no other lesson than the First), confirms the impression that he did entertain some expectation of the kind. If so, we can the more easily comprehend that he should throw himself into that position in the manner we have already endeavoured to explain. But it is not easy to see why an expectation of the kind, though proved by the event to be false, should weaken our confidence in the general inspiration under which he wrote. That inspiration did not extend to the times and the seasons when the events connected with the Second Coming would occur. Our Lord Himself said of His Coming: " But of that day or that hour knoweth no one, not even the angels in heaven, neither the Son, but the Father " (Mark xiii. 32). Even after His Resurrection, and when commissioning His Apostles to their work, He said: " It is not for you to know times or seasons, which the Father hath set within

His own authority" (Acts i. 7). To suppose that inspiration ought to have included such knowledge is to suppose that Christ Himself was not inspired. On the other hand, if St. Paul and the Christians of those days did not know when the Second Coming would take place, what could they expect but that it would be immediate? Let us place ourselves in their position. Let us be persecuted, afflicted, tormented, with no prospect before us in this world but a daily dying. Let us then remember the " blessed hope " of the return of Him on whom the most ardent affections of our souls are fixed ; and who, when He does return, will bring us freedom from all our troubles, rest from all our enemies, and eternal joy in His own immediate presence. Let us dwell on these things till our hearts, like those of the two disciples on the way to Emmaus, burn within us, till already the darkness of the present vanishes and the glory of the future is around us, and what other idea can we entertain but that in all probability Christ will come before we die? We shall not think of ourselves as doomed to die. The grave will not be the termination of the vista down which we look into the future. We shall see the Lord's chariot of glory already appearing and rapidly approaching: and the natural language of our lips will be, " Come quickly, Lord Jesus." The dead are dead, and shall soon awake. We shall be changed. Let us admit that St. Paul expected not to die, and we may still urge that his inspiration, in any just sense of the word, is not weakened because the expectation was not fulfilled.

All this then the Apostle declares to be " a mystery " (ver. 51). It would seem that the word is not to be applied to the raising of the dead. It is applied only to the changing of the living, and perhaps to their being presented, along with Christians raised from the dead, in one blessed company to their Lord. This supposition is involved in the meaning of the term upon which, as used in the New Testament, there is general agreement. It is used to signify a truth unknown before, but now made known by positive revelation. In this sense it could scarcely be applied to the raising of dead Christians. Christ was risen : these must rise with Him. Their resurrection was a logical inference from accomplished and acknowledged fact, rather than a revelation. But the other half of the statement, that the living shall be changed in a moment, in the twinkling of an eye, at the last trump, and that then both sections of the great Christian army shall be " caught up in the clouds to meet the Lord in the air, and so shall we ever be with the Lord " (1 Thess. iv. 17),—that was a revelation, a statement of the future, of things which " eye saw not, and ear heard not, and which entered not into the heart of man, but unto us God revealed them through the Spirit " (1 Cor. ii. 9, 10). We complain of the darkness of the future, and in many respects it is dark. On one point we have light. Why do we so often forget it ? " He that cometh shall come, and shall not tarry " (Heb. x. 37). He will come " to be glorified in His saints, and to be marvelled at in all them that believe" (2 Thess. i. 10); and every true member of His body shall be with Him. However long they may have slept in their graves, in whatever uttermost parts of the earth or of the sea they dwell when the trumpet sounds, not one of them shall be lost. Provision has been made for all, and we may " comfort one another with these words."

" For this corruptible must put on incorruption, and this mortal must put on immortality. But when this corruptible shall have put on incorruption, and this mortal shall have put on immortality, then shall come to pass the saying that is written, Death is swallowed up in victory. O death, where is thy victory? O death, where is thy sting? The sting of death is sin; and the power of sin is the law: but thanks be to God, which giveth us the victory through our Lord Jesus Christ. Wherefore, my beloved brethren, be ye steadfast, unmoveable, always abounding in the work of the Lord, forasmuch as ye know that your labour is not vain in the Lord."—1 COR. xv. 53-58. [R.V.]

Chapter xii.

WITH the preceding verse of the chapter the great assembly marking the day of the Lord's Coming had been convened. The last trumpet had sounded, the dead had been raised incorruptible, and the living had been changed. Everything was thus ready for that song of triumph even now in the mind of the Apostle, and soon to burst from his lips. But, before he sings the song, he must pause for a moment to behold, in this wonderful gathering of redeemed souls in glorified bodies, the contrast to the present state of things on earth, and to show that that contrast, in all its brightness, was nothing more than the accomplishment of the Divine plan: "For this corruptible must put on incorruption, and this mortal must put on immortality." It is certainly a question whether these words may not be intended only to give fresh utterance to the principle enunciated in ver. 50: "Flesh and blood cannot inherit the kingdom of God, neither doth corruption inherit incorruption;" and this seems to be the view generally entertained.[1]

[1] Comp. Hofmann, Rückert, Edwards, Ellicott.

In that case, as ver. 50 referred to none but believers alive at the *Parousia*, the same reference would need to be given to the words before us, and both clauses of ver. 53 will have to be understood of one and the same class of persons. The probabilities of the case seem to be against this view.

There is no need to repeat a principle already stated with sufficient clearness, and it is highly natural that St. Paul, before uttering the language which celebrates the completeness of the Christian victory, should think once more of all who, in any part of the argument of this chapter, have been before his mind as conquerors in the strife, and not of one class of them alone. If so, ver. 53 will contain a reference not only to such believers as shall be alive at the *Parousia*, but to such believers also as have died before that event. The two clauses will then be best understood as relating to the two classes of believers in the order in which they have been mentioned in the chapter : the first, "this corruptible," applying to Christians who have died, but shall at the great day of judgment be introduced to new and more glorious forms of life; the second, "this mortal," applying to those who, without passing through death, shall be in that day changed. Nor does the verb "put on" (ἐνδύσασθαι) appear to be less suitable to that receiving of a new body which is to be the portion of believers who have passed through the grave than to that transformation of their old bodies which shall be experienced by Christians who are alive when the Lord comes again. It can hardly be shown that the words of 2 Corinthians v. 2-4 are inconsistent with this idea. When St. Paul uses the same verb in that passage, it is not clear that he speaks only of the living. He seems to speak also of the dead, for at the beginning of the chapter he mentions " the earthly house of our tabernacle to be dissolved;" and Edwards, while making the word as employed in the passage before us refer only to the living, says of it as used in the quotation now given from the second Epistle to the same Church : " It is this personal exultation at the prospect of living to the day of Christ that the Apostle corrects in the pathetic language of his second epistle, when he sees the outward man perishing, and intimates the probability of the earthly house being dissolved (comp. 2 Cor. iv. 16 to v. 10)."[1] On the whole, therefore, it would appear as if the " corruptible " of ver. 53 were to be understood of those who die before the *Parousia*, and the " mortal " of those who live on to that great event.

The purpose or plan of God is now regarded as fulfilled, and the Apostle hastens on to take his stand upon the field where all has been accomplished, that there, in the very presence of the apparent conquerors, he may lift up his shout of triumph. " But when this corruptible shall have put on incorruption, and this mortal shall have put on

[1] On 1 Cor. xv. 53.

immortality, then," etc. Of the various reading here, which omits the words "this corruptible shall have put on incorruption," it is hardly necessary to speak. The sense is in no degree affected, and the conclusions of different critical editors appear to have been mainly determined by the views taken by them of the question whether the words "corruptible" and "mortal" in the previous verse refer to two different classes or to the same class. Refer them to the same class, and there is no need for both clauses; refer them to different classes, and the repetition is natural. External authority, too, is in this case in favour of the longer, rather than the shorter reading.

At the moment therefore, the Apostle now exclaims, when the great result shall have been at last attained, when those who have died shall have risen from their graves clothed with their incorruptible bodies, and when those who are alive shall have been changed, "then shall come to pass the saying that is written, Death is swallowed up in victory."

The quotation is from Isaiah xxv. 8, but it cannot have been taken from the LXX. as we have it, since it reads now, with an entirely different and even opposite sense, κατέπιεν ὁ θάνατος ἰσχύσας, "death, having prevailed, swallowed up." The probability is however that there is some corruption of the text; for, thus read, the clause has no connexion whatever with its context. Aquila read καταποντίσει τὸν θάνατον εἰς νῖκος,[1] and St. Paul obviously and correctly understood the Hebrew in that sense. The prophet is describing the glories of the Messianic age,— the removal at that time of all the evils from which man suffers in his present state, the introduction of all the blessings for which he longs. Among the former is death, and therefore it is said, " He shall swallow up death for ever." The same figure is met with in 2 Corinthians v. 4, and in a connexion similar to that here supplied, " That what is mortal may be swallowed up of life" (ἵνα καταποθῇ τὸ θνητὸν ὑπὸ τῆς ζωῆς); and again, in Hebrews xi. 29, the Egyptians are said to have been swallowed up in the Red Sea (κατεπόθησαν). Complete destruction is thus denoted by the word. Death shall be no more. The words εἰς νῖκος of the quotation are also interesting. The Hebrew represented by them is usually rendered by εἰς νῖκος in Greek, and by " for ever " in English : " Shall the sword devour for ever ? " (2 Sam. ii. 26); " And he kept " (said of Edom) " his wrath for ever " (Amos i. 11); and it is possible that in the instance before us St. Paul understood it in this sense. No better meaning indeed could well be afforded, " Death is swallowed up for ever." Yet the recurrence of the word νῖκος in ver. 57, with its undeniable sense of "victory" there, seems to show that the Apostle understood it in a similar sense here. That sense is also peculiarly appropriate to the whole tone of the passage, and may even be said to be the most suitable

[1] Turpie, *Old Testament in the New*, p. 134.

introduction to what follows. There has been a victory; but, O Death, that victory is not thine; it is ours: and in thy destruction our victory is declared.

Then the Apostle bursts forth into his triumphant song, "O death, where is thy victory? O death, where is thy sting?" Again it will be observed that the readings of the Textus Receptus have been departed from, but, it may be added, with universal consent. No later editor of the New Testament doubts that, on what Bishop Ellicott calls "clearly preponderating authority,"[1] the order of the clauses ought to be different from that in the Authorized Version, and that "death" ought to be substituted for "Hades" or "grave" in the second clause. "O death, where is thy victory? O death, where is thy sting?"

Death had seemed until now to have the victory. It had exercised its sway not only from Adam to Moses, but from Moses to the days of the Apostle. Through all the successive generations that had come and gone since the beginning of the world the tokens of its power had been seen. According to St. Paul's expression elsewhere, it had "reigned" (Rom. v. 14); *i.e.* it had not only been master of the fate of man, but it had also reigned like an unfeeling, tyrannical, and cruel king. It had spared neither age nor sex; it had cut down the nobly born not less than the humble, the powerful not less than the weak, the brightest ornaments of refined society not less than

[1] *Commentary on* 1 *Corinthians* in loc.

those who spread around them misery and crime. The richest, the fairest, the most highly gifted, the most loving, and the most loved had sunk into the dust at its command. Its conquest too had been complete. The eye gleaming the one moment with life and with affection was the next moment insensible to every impression that earth had been wont to make upon it; the voice that had adapted itself to every variety of human passion was hushed into a silence that no entreaty for one more utterance could break; the hand once so mobile and warm was motionless and chill. Nay, not only had there been victory on the part of death, and that victory complete, the victory had been also cruel. Taking man from this world, from all that he had valued and that had sweetened his existence, it might have been thought that death would at least be gentle, if at the same time irresistible, in its sway, and that it would smooth as much as possible a passage out of life that at the best could only lead to desolation and darkness. The contrary had been the case. In the very moment of triumph death had seemed to gloat over the miseries of its victims. It had employed every form of torture to accomplish its purpose—the wounds of the battle-field, exposure on the trackless ocean, fire and hunger and thirst, excruciating pains that had so racked the body as to deprive it of one moment's rest, and slow, lingering agony, far worse for the sufferer to bear or for his friends to witness than the one final blow that in an instant might have ended all. It had listened also to no prayer, and had yielded to no effort, to delay its coming. No money had ever bribed it, no tears softened it, no despair moved it. Oh, what a victory had that of death been ! The Apostle beheld it in the full comprehensiveness and mercilessness of its sweep. As he travelled back in thought through the ages of the past, there was no spot upon which he set his foot that did not sound hollow beneath him ; there was no corner of the earth's surface from which the voice of a weeping that refused to be comforted did not rise.

But again he looked abroad, and all was changed. Gathered together in one vast assembly were the multitudes whom death could no more touch ; one part of them risen from their graves in glorified bodies, another part so changed that they needed not to pass through the grave in order to be fit companions for those who had been " raised incorruptible." He beheld—for the unredeemed are not in his thoughts —death for them destroyed and prostrate at their feet ; and he exclaims, " O death, where is thy victory ? " (ver. 55a).

More, however, he must say ; for he remembered what a powerful weapon death had used to accomplish its end, and, lo ! that weapon too was for ever blunted and made useless. Therefore he cries again, " O death, where is thy sting ? " (ver. 55b).

We must not think of this " sting " here as a goad or prick within the conscience of the sinner, troubling him in the hour when he comes to die, and, even long before that hour, whenever he does not succeed in hardening himself against it, making him all his life "subject to bondage" (Heb. ii. 15). The word may be used with this thought of a mere goad underlying it in Acts xxvi. 14, when it was said to Saul, "It is hard for thee to kick against the goads," although even there it ought to be remembered that the goad is iron. But here it would seem, both from the context, and from the fact that St. Paul is moulding his words upon the Septuagint translation of Hosea xiii. 14, "Where, O death, is thy judgment? where, O Hades, is thy sting?" that we must understand it in its strongest sense. As such it expresses the sting of a poisonous animal like the scorpion, which carries torment that leads to death along with it (comp. Rev. ix. 10). When, accordingly, the question is asked, " O death, where is thy sting?" our attention is not directed to the human victim of death, or of the fear of death, as he recalls his transgressions and trembles in the thought of judgment, but to death itself, with its dart in its hand, first raging over the field, and then not only prostrate, but the dart fallen from its grasp and lying useless by its side.

St. Paul has been speaking figuratively, but even the figure of death with its poison-sting will hardly express all that is in his mind, and hence he hastens onward to the words of the following verse: "The sting of death is sin; and the strength of sin is the law" (ver. 56). The truths contained in these two clauses were among those upon which, in his teaching, the Apostle was most accustomed to dwell. We may look at them for a moment, and then at the purpose for which they are here referred to.

(a) "The sting of death is sin." It is the Apostle's constant lesson. When in this very chapter we read, "By man came death," and "in Adam all die" (vers. 21, 22), he obviously refers to sinful man and sinful Adam, although to have mentioned this would have diverted attention from the point then immediately in view. Still more clearly is the thought expressed in other passages: "For if by the trespass of the one death reigned through the one;" "What fruit had ye at that time in the things whereof ye are now ashamed? for the end of these things is death;" "The wages of sin is death" (Rom. v. 17; vi. 21, 23). The Jew felt powerfully that there was nothing more alien to the nature of God than death. God was the living God, and life was what He had appointed for man. Not indeed in the first instance necessarily perfect life; for in perfect life the spirit must be the one supreme influence, all the behests of which the body must implicitly and unresistingly obey. The condition of the body of man, even in his best estate, prevented this. At the moment of his creation, therefore, man could not stand at the highest point of the development he was designed to reach. But, if he continued obedient, there was nothing before him inconsistent with the full manifestation of God's loving will. There was thus no death before him. There was training, discipline, education, of one kind or another, by which he would have been brought nearer to the perfection for which he was designed. Only if he sinned would this training be interrupted —" In the day thou eatest thereof thou shalt surely die "—and death would then be due not to God, but to sin. Can we not sympathise with this even now? Many say that death is rest from toil, relief from trouble, freedom from pain of body and disappointment of spirit. True; but toil and trouble and pain and disappointment are as unnatural as death. They are its followers. "All our woe" accompanies it. How terrible, then, the sin of which it is the consequence! Not the moral evil of sin, but the dire nature of the evil that it brings on man, is in the Apostle's mind. The scorpion's sting distils no poison; inflicts no curse on man, like the poison, the curse of death.

(b) "The strength of sin is the law." Let us compare the words of the same Apostle in another passage: "Sin is not imputed when there is no law" (Rom. v. 13). It is not of the fact that the law discovers or even provokes sin that St. Paul speaks either there or here. What he dwells upon is the thought that the law is the "strength," or rather the power, of sin. If sin be the poisoned arrow discharged from the bow of death, the force that sends the arrow home and makes it penetrate the life of man so as to bring him to the grave, is the law. St. Paul is looking at the law in all the breadth with which it embraces, in all the sharpness with which it cuts into, the human heart. He sees in it the expression of the will of God, and no one has successfully resisted His will. Like the thunder of Sinai, he hears the twang of death's bow; like the lightning that flashed around the mountain he sees the arrow shot by death go swift and straight to its mark. "The sting of death is sin, and the strength of sin is the law."

(c) And now what is the special purpose of these clauses? It is to bring out how great had been the victory of death, and how much greater, in consequence, the victory gained for the believer over death. We shall go wholly astray if we imagine that St. Paul is taking us into the inner chambers of the soul, and showing us that law-work there by which the law awakens the consciousness of sin, and the consciousness of sin awakens the spirit of bondage and fear. He is looking at things in a more outward way, but at the same time on a larger scale. As he does so, death is the first great fact by which he is arrested. He acknowledges the terror with which, in itself, as the simple dissolution of life, it inspires man. But, terrible as it was, it did not stand alone in the war it had never ceased to wage, in the victories which, until met by One stronger, it had never ceased to win. It was backed by an earlier enemy, sin; and sin again was backed by that holy law of God, with its voice of condemnation most fitly expressed by winds that rend the mountains, by fire, and thunder, and earthquake. Death, sin, the law! The three go together, and cannot be separated from one another. But for sin there would have been no death: but for law there would have been no power in sin to kill. Law brings sin to its bar, and with all the force of a Divine majesty compels it to condemn its own worshippers. Sin commits the execution of the sentence to death, and death is the penalty the sinner pays. What a victory would have been the victory of death could death have made it sure ! What a monument would death have reared !—the desolation caused by the violation of the law of God the pedestal of the pillar; out of it sin rising rampant and spreading everywhere; on the top death crowned with triumph.

But victory is not given to death. Even over so great a foe victory is given to believers: "But thanks be to God, which giveth us the victory through our Lord Jesus Christ" (ver. 57). If we ask, What is meant by the description, "our Lord Jesus Christ?" it would seem as if the answer were at hand. The humiliation and death of the Redeemer are included. They belong to the appellation, "Jesus Christ:" "Jesus," the human name; "Christ," the Anointed One, the Saviour commissioned and qualified by the Father for His work of suffering and death on behalf of man. But the Resurrection and eternal life at the right hand of God are also included. They belong to the appellation, "Lord." And this last comes first, because St. Paul had been called to the Apostleship in a manner different from that of the other members of the Apostolic band. He had not, like them, been first brought to faith by companionship with his Lord's earthly life. He had first believed in the risen and glorified Lord. Let the following words of Dr Matheson, in his eloquent and deeply interesting work on *The Spiritual Development of St. Paul*, illustrate this:

"But to my mind the passage on this subject which of all others most trenchantly illustrates Paul's position is his remarkable aspiration contained in his letter to the Church of Philippi : ' That I may know Him, and the power of His resurrection, and the fellowship of His sufferings.' I have called it a remarkable aspiration, because it seems to invert the natural order. Why did not Paul say, ' that I may know Him, and the fellowship of His sufferings, and the power of His resurrection ? ' Is not this the historical arrangement in which the events of the life of Jesus actually presented themselves ? Undoubtedly it is. But it is not the order in which the events of the life of Jesus presented themselves to Paul's experience ; that which was last, to him came first. The passage has a biographical ring in it. It tells us that Christ had come to the man of Tarsus in the inverted order of His own life. To the primitive disciples the Christian revelation had presented itself in its natural and historical order : first the Man ; then the fellowship with His sufferings ; and, last of all, the power of His resurrection. To Paul the Christian revelation presented itself in exactly the opposite arrangement ; it began with the crown, and it went back to the cross. Paul's vision rested first of all on that which was supernatural and superhuman, and he had thence to retrace his steps into that which was earthly and historical ; he began with the ' power of the resurrection,' he passed next into ' fellowship with the sufferings,' and he ended with the recognition of that which identified Christ with humanity. His spiritual life was in one sense a progress from Damascus to Galilee ; it had to find its terminus where that of Peter and John had found its beginning. Its goal was to be the discovery of that perfect bond of humanity which bound the heart of the disciple to the heart of the Master ; and in reaching that discovery it attained the completion of its journey precisely where the first Apostles had begun " (p. 41).

Once more: the word "our" brings out the personal appropriation of Christ in the unity of faith. In the background, therefore, of the Apostle's thoughts it may be said that there lies the idea of a complete redemption; but only in the background. The main thought is still, as it has all along been, victory over death. To that victory it may be said that every element of redemption in its widest sense belongs. Death is the highest expression of man's "corruption," "dishonour," and "weakness." We behold in it the most striking token of his defeat and fall. Victory over it thus includes victory over everything that brings condemnation, or degradation, or misery. Death is the "last" enemy. When it has been bound, banished, destroyed, there has been given us a victory over every other spiritual foe, and not over it alone.

The Christian victory is won. Before we part from it, let us fix our minds a little more fully upon the thought that it is a "*victory*" of which St. Paul has spoken. The Christian, if he must die, enters the valley of the shadow of death, not as one who is submitting to the inevitable, but as a conqueror. Most men can submit in their last hours to God, and can lie down to die without trying to rebel against the strong hand which has them in its grasp with a power that they would vainly endeavour to shake off. "When a man," it has been said, "feels that there is no help, and he must go, he lays him down to die as quietly as a tired traveller wraps himself in his cloak to sleep."[1] That is not victory; it is defeat. It is the weaker yielding to the stronger. It is saying, "O death, thou hast conquered at last: do thy worst, I contend no more." Such is not the position of the Christian as here contemplated. With him rather the victory remains. "All things" are his, and among these "death" is his (1 Cor. iii. 22).

Now therefore we may adopt the practical conclusion added by St. Paul to everything he had said: "Wherefore, my beloved brethren, be ye steadfast, unmovable, always abounding in the work of the Lord, inasmuch as ye know that your labour is not vain in the Lord" (ver. 58). It is unnecessary to suppose, as has been sometimes done, that the first two expressions met with in these words, "steadfast" and "unmovable," refer to doctrine, the third, "abounding," to active exertion, as if the words "in the work of the Lord" were to be connected only with the one mentioned last. Had the Apostle intended this difference, he would undoubtedly have brought it out more clearly. But there was no need to direct our thoughts to any such distinction between belief and practice. To St. Paul's mind the two constituted one whole. There could be no genuine belief which was not followed by corresponding practice. There could be no Christian practice which did not rest upon the facts of the person and the life of Christ. Doctrine is as dis-

[1] Robertson, *Sermons*, vol. iii.

tinctly implied in the mention of "the work of the Lord" as though it had been expressly named. To be "steadfast" and "unmovable" in good works is as much required of the Christian as to display these qualities in regard to doctrine; while to be "abounding" in our love and appreciation of doctrine is as necessary as to be abounding in work. In these circumstances it seems best to connect all the three adjectives with the same subject, "the work of the Lord."

All of them express ideas of their own. "Steadfast" connects itself with the thought of a building reared upon a good foundation, a building settled and firm (comp. Col. i. 23). "Unmovable" connects itself with the thought of movement occasioned by outward causes—storms or earthquakes in the case of a building, heresies or temptations of any kind in the case of Christian men (comp. Col. i. 23). "Abounding," again, reminds us that our Christian life is not to be a stunted growth; that the Christian does not ask himself how little, but how much he can do for the Lord who has redeemed him by His blood; and that, forgetting the things that are behind, he constantly presses onward to those that are before. This last note of their high calling is that in which the followers of Jesus are even more apt to fail than in either steadfastness or unmovableness; and therein may lie the reason why the Apostle gives it peculiar emphasis by placing the word "always" before it. Certainly for no aspect of their life do Christians stand more in need of the voice of exhortation. They fail to think enough, not simply of "the blessing of the gospel of Christ," but of "the fulness" of its blessing (Rom. xv. 29). Into the depths of the love which has been revealed to them they do not seek to penetrate. To the heights of the glory to which they may be brought they make no effort to ascend. With the boundless treasures that are before them they do not care to be enriched. They have passed, it may be, the line which separates death from life and hell from heaven. They are out of the wilderness, delivered from its trials; and there, therefore, they will rest from their labours. The pleasant land that is before them they will explore no further; and already, on this side of Jordan, they would pitch their tents, and be at peace.

Nor is this spirit less apt to display itself in relation to the duties than in relation to the privileges of the Christian life. Too often in Christian living, even when thoroughly sincere, there is a want of largeness of heart, of freedom of spirit, of those ever loftier flights with which they that wait upon the Lord ought like eagles to mount into the air (Isa. xl. 31). One would think that the spirit of the Old Testament must in this respect have been not unfrequently higher than ours. We too seldom speak of "running" the way of God's commandments, when He shall "enlarge" our hearts (Ps. cxix. 32). We too seldom hear the song: "O Lord, truly I am Thy servant: I am Thy servant, the son of Thine handmaid; Thou hast loosed my bonds. I will offer to Thee the sacrifice of thanksgiving, and will call upon the name of the Lord. . . . Praise ye the Lord" (Ps. cxvi. 16, 17, 19). Perhaps it is not difficult to explain why it should be so. The Israelite of old dwelt in the presence of God, although that God was less fully revealed to him than to us in the more attractive features of His character. God was in the midst of Israel. The devout Jew could always lift his eyes to the temple on Mount Moriah and sing, "In Salem also is His tabernacle, and His dwelling-place in Zion" (Ps. lxxvi. 2). He knew that his Friend, his Protector, his Shield in the day of battle, his Tower of defence against any besieging foe, was always at hand, and ready to deliver him. His spirits, therefore, could always rise in adversity, and he could "abound in hope." Christian men often fail to have this deep sense of the immediate presence of their Father and Redeemer. Their minds are occupied with the process by which the work of their redemption was carried through at the time when Jesus was on earth. They accompany Him who loved them and gave Himself for them to the successive scenes of toil and suffering and agony and death through which He passed when He tabernacled in the flesh. They go in search of Him, and do not sufficiently realize that He has come, and that He is always coming, in search of them. Their Christian graces and privileges are not nourished, to the extent at least that they ought to be, by the light of the countenance of a present and a living Lord.

It is quite otherwise with the New Testament itself, and with the displays of feeling that are brought under our notice there. In particular, that we may keep close to the passage which we are now considering, it is so with St. Paul in the words before us. The work "of the Lord" he says, and again he speaks of labour not vain "in the Lord;" and there cannot be a moment's doubt that by "the Lord," thus twice mentioned, he means Jesus Christ, not merely in His earthly life, but in His exalted and heavenly life. That glorified Lord was continually by His people's side, knowing them, sympathising with them, making His grace sufficient for them, and perfecting His strength in their weakness. Therefore might they always be steadfast, always be unmovable, always abound. He that was with them was far more than all that could be against them.

Finally, also, they might look beyond this present scene, when everything they had toiled or suffered for here would bring with it its own reward. It is not a merely general reward of which St. Paul speaks, one that may be valuable in itself, but may have no correspondence to the labours previously undergone, or no intimate bond of connexion with them. The word used by him for "vain" is that used in ver. 14 of this chapter ($\kappa \epsilon \nu \acute{o} \varsigma$), and distinct in meaning from that translated by the same English term in ver. 17. It expresses not only what is vain, in that it comes to naught and produces no result, but what is in itself empty and void. That therefore which is not "vain" or "void" is that which is full, rich in substance, pregnant with results. And such is the Christian "labour" to which St. Paul refers. To the eye of the world it may seem vain. These labours for the good of others who often neither think of them nor value them when known; these self-denials and self-sacrifices to bring about, though it may be on a narrow field, a better time for the poor, the criminal, or the sorrowing; these struggles in the distant recesses of the soul and in the private chamber to rise above the world, and to gain in larger measure the spirit of that heavenly and Divine Master whom he follows, but of whom he continually falls so far short; these renouncings of earthly pleasures which he might enjoy, and of earthly riches and honours which he might gain,—all these may seem to those around the believer the outcome of a fantastic imagination or of fevered dreams. Is it possible to say that they would be more than this were there no hereafter, were there nothing but the grave before us at the end of thankless and not unfrequently disappointing toil, were there no resurrection of the dead? But they assume a new character in the light of the eternal world, and of the Resurrection of Him who died for us, and rose again that we, having partaken of His spirit, may also share His glory. They are the labours of the seedtime, to be followed by an abundant harvest. They are the battle to be crowned with victory, the race to be ended at a glorious goal, the voyage over stormy seas that the ship may reach a smiling land, and may enter an eternal haven. Even while they are endured they are full of promise and of hope, and along with each is given a foretaste of the coming blessedness. The heart rises above everything that would otherwise weaken or discourage it. We may be counted fools for Christ's sake; but in Him our weakness is strength our tears are smiles, our sorrow is joy. "It is God that justifieth ; who is he that shall condemn ? It is Christ Jesus that died, yea rather, that was raised from the dead, who is at the right hand of God, who also maketh intercession for us ; " " Let us not be weary in well-doing ; " " Our labour is not void in the Lord."

www.ingramcontent.com/pod-product-compliance
Lightning Source LLC
Chambersburg PA
CBHW070732160426
43192CB00009B/1405